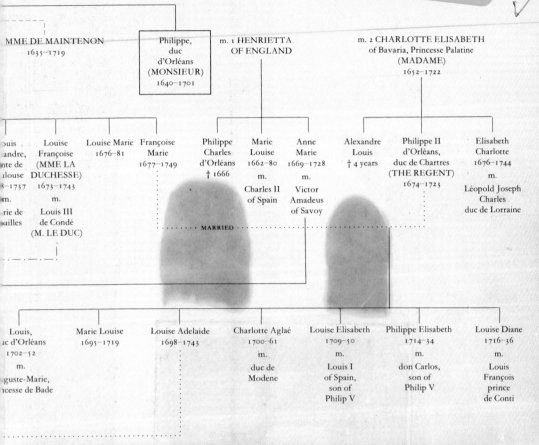

MME DE MAINTENON
1635–1719

Philippe,
duc
d'Orléans
(MONSIEUR)
1640–1701

m. 1 HENRIETTA
OF ENGLAND

m. 2 CHARLOTTE ELISABETH
of Bavaria, Princesse Palatine
(MADAME)
1652–1722

ouis
andre,
te de
louse
8–1737
m.
rie de
ailles

Louise
Françoise
(MME LA
DUCHESSE)
1673–1743
m.
Louis III
de Condé
(M. LE DUC)

Louise Marie
1676–81

Françoise
Marie
1677–1749

Philippe
Charles
d'Orléans
† 1666

Marie
Louise
1662–80
m.
Charles II
of Spain

Anne
Marie
1669–1728
m.
Victor
Amadeus
of Savoy

Alexandre
Louis
† 4 years

Philippe II
d'Orléans,
duc de Chartres
(THE REGENT)
1674–1723

Elisabeth
Charlotte
1676–1744
m.
Léopold Joseph
Charles
duc de Lorraine

········· MARRIED ·········

Louis,
uc d'Orléans
1702–52
m.
uguste-Marie,
ncesse de Bade

Marie Louise
1695–1719

Louise Adelaide
1698–1743

Charlotte Aglaé
1700–61
m.
duc de
Modene

Louise Elisabeth
1709–50
m.
Louis I
of Spain,
son of
Philip V

Philippe Elisabeth
1714–34
m.
don Carlos,
son of
Philip V

Louise Diane
1716–36
m.
Louis
François
prince
de Conti

The family tree

of Louis XIV

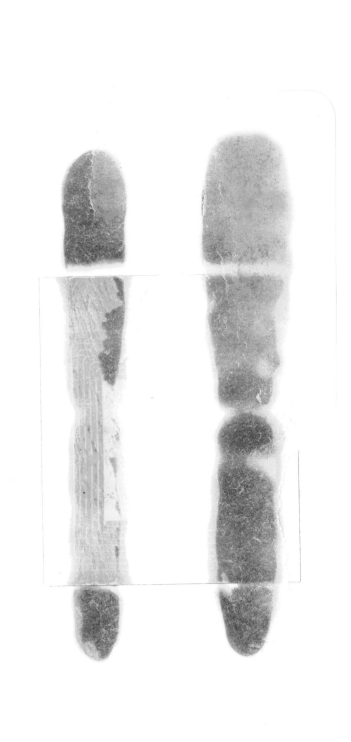

THE SUN KING
AND HIS LOVES

Frontispiece. The pursuit of glory. Louis XIV, 1673

THE SUN KING
AND HIS LOVES

Lucy Norton

Hamish Hamilton

London

Published in Great Britain 1983
by Hamish Hamilton Ltd
Garden House 57–59 Long Acre London WC2E 9JZ

© The Folio Society Limited 1982
ISBN 0–241–10907–8

*Set in eleven point Monophoto Garamond one point leaded
with American Typefounders initials for display.
Printed by Balding + Mansell Limited, Wisbech
on Silverblade Matt cartridge.*

Printed in Great Britain

CONTENTS

ACKNOWLEDGMENTS

My grateful thanks are due to my friends Betty Askwith, Christopher Sinclair-Stevenson and Michael Holroyd for their kindness, interest and help in reading and advising me upon the text, also to the staff of The Folio Society for their encouragement and patience. Lastly, to Joy Law for the skill with which she extracted from the huge mass of available material, just the kind of illustrations I most wanted.

Some Books Consulted

CHOISY, Abbé de: *Mémoires*, Utrecht 1727.

THE LETTERS OF MADAME, Princess Palatine, translated by Gertrude Scott Stevenson, London 1924.

CAYLUS, Mme de: *Souvenirs*, Paris 1806.

SÉVIGNÉ, Mme de: *Lettres*, various editions.

MAINTENON, Mme de: *Correspondance Générale*, Paris 1865.

SAINT-SIMON, Louis de Rouvroy, Duc de: *Mémoires*.

VISCONTI, Primi: *Mémoires de la Cour de Louis XIV*.

VOLTAIRE: *Le Siècle de Louis XIV*, 1751.

MAUROIS, André: *Louis XIV à Versailles*, Paris 1955.

HALDANE, Charlotte: *Madame de Maintenon*, London 1970.

NICOLSON, Harold: *The Age of Reason*, London 1960.

ILLUSTRATIONS

Picture research by Joy Law

Half title Detail from an engraving of a silver table at Versailles.
Engraving by Pierre Le Pautre (1660–1714). (*Victoria and Albert Museum*)

Frontispiece Louis XIV: 1673. Painting by Pierre Mignard (1612–95).
(*Museo Cinco di Torino*)

1. The wedding breakfast of Louis XIV and Marie Thérèse. Anonymous
engraving. (*Bibliothèque Nationale*)

2. Louis XIV as a baby: *c.* 1643. Painting by Claude Deruet (1588–1660).
(*Musée des Beaux Arts, Orléans*)

3. Marie Mancini. Painting by Jacob Ferdinand Voet (1639–1700?) in the
Gemäldegalerie, Berlin. (*Staatliche Museen Preussicher Kulturbesitz*)

4. Louis XIV with his mother, Anne of Austria, in the Chambre du Roi
at Fontainebleau on the occasion of the signing of the marriage contract between King Vladislas IV of Poland and Princess Louise Marie de Gonzaga:
1645. Engraving by Abraham Bosse (1602–76). (*Bibliothèque Nationale*)

5. Allegory of the marriage of Louis XIV and the Peace of the Pyrenees.
Painting by Claude Deruet (1588–1660) in the Musée de Versailles. (*Cliché
de Musées Nationaux*)

6. A ball at the Louvre: 1662. Drawing by Israel Silvestre (1621–91) in
the Cabinet des Dessins, the Louvre. (*Cliché de Musées Nationaux*)

7. Louise de La Vallière: *c.* 1663. Painting by Jean Nocret (1615–72) in
the Musée de Versailles. (*Cliché de Musées Nationaux*)

8. Queen Marie Thérèse: *c.* 1664. Painting by Joseph Werner
(1637–1710) in the Musée de Versailles. (*Cliché de Musées Nationaux*)

9. Louise de La Vallière as Flora. Gouache on vellum, attributed to Jean
Petitot (1607–91), in the Musée Carnavalet. (*Lauros-Giraudon*)

10. Louis XIV as a young man. Painting by Charles Le Brun (1619–90)
in the Musée de Versailles. (*Cliché de Musées Nationaux*)

11. Design for the Pyramide, one of the fountains in the gardens of
Versailles. Drawing by Charles Le Brun (1619–90). (*Bibliothèque Nationale*)

12. Nicolas Fouquet. Painting by Sébastien Bourdon (1616–71) at Vaux-
le-Vicomte. (*Lauros-Giraudon*)

13. View of the gardens at Vaux-le-Vicomte. Engraving by Israel
Silvestre (1621–91). (*Bibliothèque Nationale*)

14. View of the Grand Cascade at Vaux-le-Vicomte. Engraving by Israel
Silvestre (1621–91). (*Bibliothèque Nationale*)

15. The Menagerie at Versailles, 1663, designed by Louis Le Vau,
(1612–70). Engraving by Aveline. (*Bibliothèque Nationale*)

16. Camels. Sketches by Charles Le Brun (1619–90) in the Cabinet des Dessins, the Louvre. (*Cliché de Musées Nationaux*)

17. André Le Nôtre. Painting by Carlo Maratta (1625–1713) in the Musée de Versailles. (*Cliché de Musées Nationaux*)

18. Perspective view of the palace and gardens of Versailles from the Place d'Armes: 1668. Painting by Pierre Patel (*c.* 1620–76) in the Musée de Versailles. (*Cliché de Musées Nationaux*)

19. The building of Versailles. Painting by Antoine François van der Meulen (1632–90) in Buckingham Palace. (*By gracious permission of Her Majesty the Queen*)

20. Indian, Turkish and Roman horsemen, with Louis XIV at their head as a Roman emperor, in the Place du Carrousel in 1662. Engravings by Jacques Bailly (*c.* 1629–79). (*Bibliothèque Nationale*)

21. Anne of Austria, Louis XIV's mother. Painting by Pierre Mignard (1612–95) in the Musée Condé at Chantilly. (*Lauros-Giraudon*)

22. Louis XIV as Apollo: 1654? Water-colour with gold on vellum by Henri Gissey (1621?–1673) in Windsor Castle. (*By gracious permission of Her Majesty the Queen*)

23. Procession of the king. The first day of the Pleasures of the Enchanted Isle. Engraving by Israel Silvestre (1621–91). (*The Elisha Whittelsey Fund, Metropolitan Museum of Art*)

24. The firework display. The third day of the Pleasures of the Enchanted Isle. Engraving by Israel Silvestre (1621–91). (*Bibliothèque Nationale*)

25. Groves of Versailles: the three fountains. Painting by Jean Cotelle (1642–1708), in the Musée de Versailles. (*Lauros-Giraudon*)

26. The siege of Lille: 1667. Painting by Antoine François van der Meulen (1632–90) in the Musée de Versailles. (*Cliché de Musées Nationaux*)

27. The siege of Tournai. Painting by Robert Bonnard (1652–after 1729), after Van der Meulen and Le Brun, in the Musée de Versailles. (*Cliché de Musées Nationaux*)

28. Jean Baptiste Colbert. Painting by Claude Lefèbvre (1632–75) in the Musée de Versailles. (*Cliché de Musées Nationaux*)

29. The Duchesse de Montpensier, la Grande Mademoiselle. Painting of the school of Mignard in the Musée de Versailles. (*Cliché de Musées Nationaux*)

30. The entry of Louis XIV and the queen into Douai: 1667. Drawing by Charles Le Brun (1619–90) in the Musée de Versailles. (*Cliché de Musée Nationaux*)

31. Madame de Sévigné: *c.* 1665. Painting by Claude Lefèbvre (1632–75). (*Musée Carnavalet*)

32. Queen Marie Thérèse. Painting by Jean François de Troy (1679–1752) in the Musée de Versailles. (*Cliché de Musées Nationaux*)

33. Madame de Montespan in her château of Clagny. Painting by an unknown artist. (*Uffizi, Florence*)

34. View of the château of Versailles showing the two new wings designed by Mansart. Engraving by Israel Silvestre (1621–91) in the Musée de Versailles. (*Cliché de Musées Nationaux*)

35. Jules Hardouin Mansart. Painting by Jean François de Troy (1679–1752) in the Musée de Versailles. (*Cliché de Musées Nationaux*)

36. Louis XIV before the château of Versailles showing the Orangery. Painting by Jean Baptiste Martin (1659–1735) in Windsor Castle. (*By gracious permission of Her Majesty the Queen*)

37. The château and garden of Clagny: 1679. Engraving by Adam Perelle (1640–95). (*Lauros-Giraudon*)

38. Silk tapestry woven for the king's barge by the Atelier de Dupont. In the Louvre, Paris. (*Cliché de Musées Nationaux*)

39. Madame de Maintenon and her niece. Painting by Ferdinand Elle (1648–1717) in the Musée de Versailles. (*Alinari-Giraudon, at the Mansell Collection*)

40. The ballet of the Festival of Eros and Bacchus, by Lulli, performed before the royal family in the Petit Parc at Versailles. Engraving by Le Pautre. (*Roger Viollet*)

41. Louis XIV attending a lesson given by Bossuet to the Dauphin. Painting by an unknown artist. (*Roger Viollet*)

42. Madame de Montespan with her children, the Duc du Maine, the Comte du Vexin, Mademoiselle de Nantes and Mademoiselle de Tours. Painting after Mignard in the Musée de Versailles. (*Cliché de Musées Nationaux*)

43. Louis XIV: 1670. Pastel by Robert Nanteuil (1623–78). (*Uffizi, Florence*)

44. The siege of Maastricht. Painting by an unknown artist, seventeenth-century French school, in the Musée de Versailles. (*Cliché de Musées Nationaux*)

45. The battle near the Bruges canal: 1667. Painting after van der Meulen in the Musée de Versailles. (*Cliché de Musées Nationaux*)

46. Entry of Louis XIV and Marie Thérèse into Arras: 1667. Painting by Antoine François van der Meulen (1632–90) in the Musée de Versailles. (*Cliché de Musées Nationaux*)

47. A lampoon on Madame de Maintenon, the Widow Scarron. Anonymous. (*Bibliothèque Nationale*)

48. Madame de Maintenon at prayer: 1697. Engraving by Claude Auguste Berey (*fl.* 1690–1730). (*Bibliothèque Nationale*)

49. Anne de Rohan-Chabot, Princesse de Soubise. Painting attributed to Beaubrun in the Musée de Versailles. (*Cliché de Musées Nationaux*)

50. The Duchesse de Fontanges. Painting by Jean François de Troy (1697–1752). (*Robert Harding Picture Library*)

51. Madame de Montespan. Painting by Pierre Mignard (1612–95) in the Musée de Berry, Bourges. (*Lauros-Giraudon*)

52. The king in Flanders. Engraving by Jean Langlois (1649–1712). (*Bibliothèque Nationale*)

53. View of the grove of the Arc de Triomphe in the garden of Versailles. Gouache by Jean Cotelle (1642–1708) in the Galerie du Grand Trianon, Musée de Versailles. (*Cliché de Musées Nationaux*)

54. The earliest of Le Nôtre's garden schemes for Versailles: 1677. (*Bibliothèque Nationale*)

55. The silver throne-room at Versailles. Engraving by Berain in the Musée de Versailles. (*Cliché de Musées Nationaux*)

56. Charles Le Brun. Bust by Antoine Coysevox (1640–1720) in the Wallace Collection, London. (*The Wallace Collection*)

57. Audience given by Louis XIV to the Comte de Fuentes, ambassador of the King of Spain: 1662. Tapestry woven for Versailles at the Atelier Gobelins, in the Musée de Versailles. (*Cliché de Musées Nationaux*)

58. The queen's mausoleum at St Germain des Près: 1683. Engraving by Antoine Benoist (1632–1717). (*Bibliothèque Nationale*)

59. The hall of mirrors, the *Galerie de Glaces*, at Versailles. Engraving by J. M. Chevotet, after Herisset, in the Musée de Versailles. (*Cliché de Musées Nationaux*)

60. Madame de Maintenon. Painting after Mignard in the Musée de Versailles. (*Cliché de Musées Nationaux*)

61. Two pages from Masse's Atlas, *Traité de l'Attaque*, showing the building of fortifications and used by Louis in his wars in Flanders. In the Bibliothèque du Service Technique du Génie. (*Lauros-Giraudon*)

62. Louis XIV in armour. Painting by Hyacinthe Rigaud (1659–1743) in the Musée de Versailles. (*Cliché de Musées Nationaux*)

63. Louis XIV playing billiards in the third chamber: 1694. Engraving by Trouvain. (*Lauros-Giraudon*)

64. *Bal à la Françoise*; Louis XIV dancing at Versailles: 1682. Anonymous engraving. (*Lauros-Giraudon*)

65. Still life with silver. Painting by Alexandre François Desportes (1661–1743). (*Mary Wetmore Shively Bequest, Metropolitan Museum of Art*)

66. The Grand Trianon: 1724. Painting by Pierre Denis Martin (*c.* 1663–1742) in the Musée de Versailles. (*Cliché de Musées Nationaux*)

67. A design for the gardens at Marly. (*Archives Nationales*)

68. General view of Marly. Engraving by Pierre Aveline (1620–1722) at Marly. (*Roger Viollet*)

69. The water-pumping machine at Marly. Painting by Pierre Denis Martin (*c.*1663–1740) in the Musée de Versailles. (*Cliché de Musées Nationaux*)

70. The Triumph of Flora. Painting by Nicolas Poussin (1594–1665): part of the king's collection, now in the Louvre. (*Cliché de Musées Nationaux*)

71. The Duc de Bourgogne. Painting by Hyacinthe Rigaud (1659–1743) in the Musée de Versailles. (*Cliché de Musées Nationaux*)

72. Victor Amadeus I: *c.* 1632. Miniature painting by Giovanna Garzoni (1600–70). (*Pitti Palace, Florence*)

73. Christine, wife of Victor Amadeus I: *c.* 1632. Miniature painting by Giovanna Garzoni (1600–70). (*Pitti Palace, Florence*)

74. The Duc de Saint-Simon. Wedding portrait by an unknown artist. (*Bibliothèque Nationale*)

75. Fontainebleau—a bird's eye view of the château and park by

Francini, engraved by Lasne in 1614, in the Galerie des Certs, Fontainebleau. (*The Mansell Collection*)

76. Marie Adelaide of Savoy, the Duchesse de Bourgogne. Painting by Pierre Gobert (1662–1744) in the Musée de Versailles. (*Cliché de Musées Nationaux*)

77 & 78. Fountains in the maze and garden at Versailles. Engravings by David Le Clerc (1679–1738). (*Lucy Norton*)

79. The wedding of the Duc de Bourgogne to Marie Adelaide of Savoy: 1697. Cartoon by Antoine Dieu in 1710 for a tapestry to be made at the Gobelins, in the Musée de Versailles. (*Cliché de Musées Nationaux*)

80. View of the Bassin d'Apollon at Versailles. Painting by an unknown artist in the Musée de Versailles. (*Cliché de Musées Nationaux*)

81. Detail from a painting by Pierre Denis Martin (*c.* 1663–1742) showing Louis XIV in his wheelchair *en promenade*. In the Musée de Versailles. (*Cliché de Musées Nationaux*)

82. The siege of Namur: 1692. Painting by Pierre Denis Martin (*c.* 1663–1742) in the Musée de Versailles. (*Cliché de Musées Nationaux*)

83. The Duc d'Anjou is recognized as the future King of Spain: 1700. Anonymous engraving. (*Lauros-Giraudon*)

84. Details from an engraving showing *Le Grand Hiver*, the hard winter of 1709. Anonymous engraving. (*Bibliothèque Nationale*)

85. The family of the Grand Dauphin. Painting by Pierre Mignard (1612–95) in the Musée de Versailles. (*Cliché de Musées Nationaux*)

86. Claude Louis Hector, Duc de Villars, Maréchal of France: 1714. Painting after Rigaud in the Musée de Versailles. (*Lauros-Giraudon*)

87. Louis XIV giving audience to his subjects and judgments in their disputes. Anonymous contemporary engraving in the Musée de Versailles. (*Cliché de Musées Nationaux*)

88. The chapel at Versailles. Anonymous engraving. (*Bibliothèque Nationale*)

89. Violinist in the king's ensemble: 1688. Engraving by Nicolas Arnoult. (*Larousse*)

90. The procession preceding the signing of the Treaty of Utrecht: 1713. Anonymous engraving. (*Roger Viollet*)

91. The fifth chamber of the *appartements*. Engraving by Trouvain. (*Bibliothèque Nationale*)

92. Louis XIV with his heirs and the Duchesse de Ventadour. Painting by Nicolas de Largillière (1656–1746). (*The Wallace Collection*)

93. Cheating at cards. Seventeenth-century engraving. (*The Mansell Collection*)

94. Louis XIV at his prayers. Miniature from a Book of Hours owned by the king. (*Bibliothèque Nationale*)

95. The funeral procession of Louis XIV. Anonymous engraving. (*Bibliothèque Nationale*)

End papers Decorations taken from a design for a table to be made at the Gobelins; one very similar exists in the Louvre. Anonymous. (*Bibliothèque Nationale*)

1. The wedding breakfast of Louis XIV and Marie Thérèse, daughter of Philip IV of Spain

THE SUN KING AND
HIS LOVES

hen he had outgrown the loves of childhood, Louis XIV, in his long reign, had five grand passions; for four women, one after another, and for a house and garden which he loved the best and longest of all, giving to it an unstinting care and devotion that no woman, with the possible exception of his beloved little great-niece, Adelaide of Savoy, ever inspired in his cold and selfish heart.

Louis XIV was four years old when he ascended the throne at his father's death in 1643. He inherited many great and splendid palaces, including the Louvre, the Tuileries, Fontainebleau, Vincennes, and beautiful Saint-Germain. He also inherited his father's special treasure, a modest hunting-lodge in the desolate region near the village of Versailles, a vast tract of fenland, full of swamps and reedy ponds with here and there clumps of undergrowth and stunted trees. It was perfect country for hunting, the king's greatest pleasure, a place where horses might gallop and hounds run unobstructed for miles on end, where wolves and deer abounded and there was game of every kind.

Louis XIII had dearly loved the bright little house which his architect Le Vau had built there for him. To him it represented a haven of peace and quiet, providing for him an escape from family rows with his terrible mother, Marie de Medicis, and the reproaches of Anne of Austria, his unloved wife. The house was deliberately planned to exclude ladies, for although it contained twenty rooms, only two of them were bedrooms—a comfortable apartment for the king himself, and a large dormitory for men only. A tactful friend said that the king's intention was to provide lodging for very few followers in order to leave his repose untroubled by pestering courtiers. Louis XIII put it rather differently: 'All those ladies whom the queen takes everywhere with her would spoil everything for me.'

As the work progressed he took an ever-increasing pleasure in planning the park and garden; we read of him 'driving out from Saint-Germain in his small one-horse carriage to see to his flowerbeds and groves of saplings'. It was all turning out exactly as he had intended, modest, practical, convenient and, in addition, it had considerable charm, for it looked remarkably pretty with its combination of rose-

2. *Louis XIV as a baby*

red bricks and white stonework, and its high roof of blue slates. His courtiers called it 'the king's little house of cards', not because it appeared flimsy but because with its cheerful colours it resembled the back of a playing card. Even the interior had an elegance that was surprising in view of Louis XIII's lack of taste; but this may have been because his sister, the Duchess of Savoy,* made him a present of the complete furnishings of the four reception rooms. Woven of Genoese velvet on a silver ground, the hangings and upholstery for the first were a soft blue, for the second silver-grey, for the third and fourth green and silver respectively; and the beauty of these colours may be seen today in the decoration of the Trianon of Louis XIV.

Louis XIII's pride in the little house grew with his love for it. He went at first for the hunting alone; then we read of him, like his son in years to come, interrupting official visits to Compiègne or Saint-Germain to take his guests on personally conducted tours. On one occasion he actually kept the hunt waiting 'while he amused himself inspecting the newly arrived suites of furniture and the kitchen equipment'.

*Chrétienne de France, daughter of Henri IV and Marie de Medicis, married Victor Amadeus I, Duke of Savoy. He, by his second wife, was the grandfather of Marie Adelaide, Duchesse de Bourgogne, and later Dauphine of France.

When the chase led him far from Saint-Germain he took to staying over-night in his new house, attended by a very small following of intimate friends which usually included his most loyal and trusted favourite, the Duc de Saint-Simon, father of the great memoirist. Gradually the king's visits to Versailles became longer and more frequent, until towards the end of his life when his health had begun to fail, he seems to have imagined it becoming, as it were, a second Escorial, for he said to his confessor after recovering from a bout of illness, 'If God should spare me, as soon as I see that my dauphin has learned to ride, I shall set him in my place and retire to Versailles with four fathers of your Order, so that we may talk of holy matters and banish all other thoughts than of my soul and its salvation.'

God, however, did not spare him. In the March of that same year, 1643, he took to his bed at Saint-Germain and, summoning his first minister, made provision for his four-year-old son's long minority, entrusting Queen Anne with the regency of France and the upbringing of the little dauphin. He also advanced the date of the prince's ceremonial baptism, contending that although in years so young, he had already reached the age of reason, which would not normally have been achieved until his seventh birthday.

Accordingly, on 21 April 1643, the dauphin was taken to the chapel at Saint-Germain and there anointed with the Holy Oils, having first sworn 'with wonderful assurance' to renounce the devil and all his works. He then received the names Louis Dieudonné, the Gift of God. After that he was taken to his father's bedside and the king kissed him, asking whether he knew his name. 'Yes, Sire, Louis XIV,' came the firm reply; to which the dying king said, 'Not yet, my boy; not yet. But you will be soon, for that is the will of God.' And indeed two days later the king expired and Louis XIV's long reign had begun.

The queen-regent, Anne of Austria, so-called because although a Spanish princess she was of Hapsburg descent, now governed France with the help of Cardinal Mazarin, her first minister, intimate friend, and perhaps her lover. She took into her own hands the formation of the young king's character and his religious education. His training in statecraft and the rest of his education were made the cardinal's responsibility.

Queen Anne was deeply religious and, like most people of that period, firmly believed in the demi-deity of kings once they had been crowned and anointed with the Holy Oils. She recalled the Holy Empire and how, in the reign of her ancestor the Emperor Charles, Viennese gentlemen were made to draw the leathern blinds over their carriage windows when passing the imperial coach, lest their profane glances should fall upon the ruler's hallowed countenance.

She instilled into her son the belief that a king might do as he wished but should not forget that God would hold him personally responsible for the spiritual welfare and morals of his subjects. Her teaching took deep root in his mind for, although his confessors never considered him to be religious in any deep sense of the word, he strictly obeyed and caused his subjects to obey the rules of the established Church. As he grew old he became increasingly gripped by the fear of God, living in terror of mortal sin and eternal damnation.

From Cardinal Mazarin the young king learned of the conduct of State affairs and the method by which great decisions are made. He was eager to learn, and never in his life shirked hard and often boring work. Even in his early teens he willingly devoted two hours each morning to listening at the meetings of the privy council, where he was not allowed to say a word. But Mazarin, besides being a great statesman, was an athlete and a splendid horseman who hunted with the king and took part in many other outdoor sports. He won his pupil's admiration and gratitude, but never his hero-worship or his affection. It may be that Louis's pride could not tolerate Mazarin's intimacy with his mother, or, possibly, the cardinal's quiet ingratiating manner and his method of gaining consent by patience and persuasion did not shine in comparison with the dashing imperiousness of the boy's idol, Henri IV.

There were other ways, however, in which the influence of Mazarin had a lasting effect. He was a man of culture with an all-embracing passion for the arts, which his enormous wealth allowed him to indulge. His rooms overflowed with pictures, sculpture, tapestries and furniture of exquisite craftsmanship. He collected beautiful objects from all over the world, porcelain from China and rich silks from Italy, and very soon his pupil had begun to form collections of paintings and tapestries on his own account, several of which came from England, sold to him by Cromwell after the execution of Charles I.

For the first five years of his reign Louis XIV and Philippe, Duc d'Orléans, his younger brother, lived quietly and happily with their mother, first in the grim old palace of the Louvre, then in the brighter, airier Palais Royal, where there was a garden large enough for them to play soldiers on a grand scale, and learn shooting by potting at sparrows with miniature arquebuses. In 1648, however, when Louis was ten years old, their peace was shattered by a revolt of the *parlements* and the nobility in an attempt to regain the ancient privileges of which Cardinal Richelieu had stripped them in the previous reign. This revolt erupted in the horrible civil war known as *Les Frondes*, meaning *The Slings*, so-called after a stone-throwing war-game at that time the rage with the urchins of Paris. Had it not been for Mazarin's crafty diplomacy and Queen Anne's unshakable courage it might have ended in a revolution, but the risings were finally quelled and peace returned. Louis XIV, however, never forgot that troubled time; nor did he ever forgive the people of Paris for breaking by night into the Palais Royal and invading his bedroom in order to convince themselves that the royal family had not fled from the capital.

The civil war was in two parts, with an intermission during which the king attained his legal majority on his thirteenth birthday and nominally took the government of France into his own hands. There were then public rejoicings, with *Te Deums* in the churches, a tournament, fireworks, and the performance of a ballet, in which the king danced publicly for the first time. He was also allowed to play cards for money. Among the festivities was a great hunt at Versailles, with a breakfast at which, again for the first time, he acted as host. According to the records it was a triumphant success, for the food and wine were acclaimed delicious and the service admirable, notwithstanding that the cooks and waiters were all workers on the estate, and not servants trained in the king's household.

With the return of peace Queen Anne decided to move from the Palais Royal to the Tuileries, which had a magnificent garden designed and cared for by André Le Nôtre, the highly talented supervisor of the royal gardens. Even at the Tuileries the queen felt insecure and in danger from the Parisian rabble, and soon afterwards she moved a second time, taking her little boys to Saint-Germain which she made their home, using Le Nôtre and the king's architect François Mansart (great-uncle by marriage of the famous Jean Hardouin Mansart) who later designed the chapel and much of the château of Versailles, to replan and improve the gardens and design a magnificent scheme of decoration for the interior.

For his mother, when she did not obstruct him in his pleasures, the young king felt a tender love and admiration that remained with him for the rest of his life. He respected her genuine piety and her fearlessness. He loved her for her fastidious cleanliness (far in advance of her time), her fresh, crisp linen, her delicious scent and the sweet-smelling flowers that made the air fragrant in all her richly decorated rooms. Above all, he delighted in the happy atmosphere at her court and in the witty, laughing conversation in her circle of elegant and well-bred ladies. He loved to be with them, and long after her death, Versailles (where she never lived) was said to be pervaded by her spirit, made evident in her son's love of flowers, scented gloves, and spotless linen. To him she remained the image of perfection in a great lady and when, after his wife's death, he married for the second time and for love, he chose Mme de Maintenon who in many ways resembled her.

17

3. Marie Mancini, Cardinal Mazarin's youngest niece

None the less there were violent quarrels. As Louis passed from youth to manhood he increasingly resented his mother's supervision, more especially when she interfered with his amusements or showed her disapproval of his love affairs. But Queen Anne continued to keep a strict eye upon her son's conduct and, since women were clearly going to play an important role in his life, she watched anxiously for scandals or unacceptable attachments. It was high time for him to settle down; an early marriage appeared eminently desirable, and the king himself was not wholly averse to the idea, though it meant parting from Marie Mancini, the youngest of Mazarin's three charming nieces, with whom he had formed a romantic attachment. She was fifteen years old, gentle, lively, something of a blue-stocking, and she adored the king, while he felt for her an admiring affection that might easily have turned to passion. The queen and Mazarin were horrified by rumours that Louis might be contemplating, as indeed he was, marriage with so unsuitable a partner. Mazarin himself was against the match for political reasons, and in his letters to his former pupil stressed very forcibly his niece's unfitness by birth and temperament to be queen. Louis's mother, meanwhile, urged her son's duty to sacrifice himself for the sake of God and France, and, when he at last complied, set herself to the task of finding an eligible princess.

The choice, purely for dynastic reasons, fell upon María Teresa, the daughter of Philip IV of Spain with whom France had long been at war. Louis did not object, and after five months of difficult negotiation a peace treaty was signed. France and Spain formed an alliance and the wedding of Louis XIV and the Spanish Infanta was fixed for 9 June 1660. The place chosen for the ceremony was the Isle of Pheasants, a tiny island in the middle of the narrow River Bidassoa, which marked the boundary between France and Spain. Temporary bridges were built connecting the opposite banks, a vast marquee was erected with a division across the centre, and on this small patch of neutral ground, so arranged that neither royal party encroached by so much as the shortest step upon the other's territory, the marriage took place.

The king, incognito, had seen his bride on the previous evening and had not been favourably impressed by her appearance. He had often been heard to say that he intended to marry a beautiful woman; but María Teresa was anything but that, being short and stout ('little better than a dwarf,' said the spiteful courtiers), with a colourless complexion and a bearing that was icily stiff and proud. None the less, he said afterwards to his mother that although disappointed by her looks, he thought that given time he might come to love her. The Infanta, on the other hand, fell in love at first sight, with a possessive,

19

jealous passion which she found hard to control. 'Do not leave me, not even for a moment,' she begged him on the first day of their honeymoon; and the king accordingly gave orders that they were not to be separated on the long journey northwards to Vincennes, where they rested for a month before their state entry into Paris.

Mazarin, meanwhile, had been in poor health, suffering from gout and a stone. He was not well enough to drive in the triumphal procession through the streets of the capital, but watched it from a window in the company of Queen Anne. It was his supreme moment, the display of his statesmanship in bringing France to peace and securing for the king a powerful alliance. He received magnificent evidence of the king's gratitude, for when the golden coach containing the new queen drew level with the balcony on which he sat with Queen Anne, the king reined back his beautiful Spanish charger and, sweeping off his feathered hat, gave a deep bow, so gracefully done, so expressive of love and gratitude for his mother and his old friend that the widow Scarron, who watched from a nearby window, wrote to a friend, 'Nothing more graceful could be imagined. I think the queen will have retired last night very well pleased with the husband of her choice'—a somewhat surprising remark since, as Mme Scarron well knew, poor María Teresa had had no say in the matter. Had any fortune-teller told the future Mme de Maintenon that she had been lost in admiration of her future husband she might very probably have fainted.

During the autumn and winter of 1660 the cardinal's health continued to deteriorate. He died on 9 March 1661, at the age of fifty-nine, in the fortress of Vincennes. Queen Anne had given him most tender care throughout his long illness, and the king, when they brought him the news, burst into tears. Louis XIV was apt to weep over very small matters; but the death of Cardinal Mazarin, his godfather, tutor and true friend, shook him profoundly. For two hours, in the early morning of 10 March, he shut himself up alone in his room, and then, while it was not yet day, he summoned his first council. This was the moment for which he had been waiting; he knew exactly what he intended to do. On the following day he called a second meeting of the council and announced to his ministers and secretaries of State that Mazarin would not be replaced. 'In future', he said, 'I shall be my own first minister,' and he continued by forbidding them to seal agreements, sign official documents, or make any payments without his prior knowledge and consent.

The news was received with amazement. The king had been known to obey Mazarin implicitly; indeed, the Venetian ambassador had described him as being 'in mind and soul subordinated to the

4. *Louis with his mother, Anne of Austria, in the Chambre du Roi at Fontainebleau*

cardinal', and it was generally believed that he would immediately give the post of first minister to Nicolas Fouquet, the brilliant minister of finance. But Louis XIV had other ideas. 'I began', he wrote in his *Mémoires*, 'by casting my eye over all the different parts of the realm—not indifferently but with a master's eye, and I was deeply shocked to find that every one of them merited, nay urgently required, my personal attention.' There should, he decided, be no replacement for Mazarin, no more prelates with power in state affairs amassing vast fortunes while the king remained poor, and causing Frenchmen's loyalties to be divided between their Church and their king.

The cardinal, in his will, bequeathed the greater part of his wealth to the king, including his collections of pictures, books, furniture, and precious stones, among which were 'Les Mazarins', eighteen diamonds of enormous size. It was a millionaire's bequest; but he told the king that these costly treasures were worth nothing in comparison with the value of his personal secretary, Jean Baptiste Colbert, who now passed into the royal service and became one of the greatest statesmen in the history of France. Mazarin, at the same time, warned King Louis to beware of Fouquet—a man of insatiable ambition whose manner of living was too insolently magnificent to be attributable to honest effort in the service of his country.

21

5. Allegory of the marriage of Louis XIV and the Peace of the Pyrenees

Together with the love of power and the decision to take upon himself the absolute rule of his kingdom, the young king became infused with the desire for glory. 'The pursuit of glory', he wrote, 'requires the same sensitivity, and—dare I say it?—the same restraint as the most tender passions.' He sought for glory everywhere, in victory on the field of battle, in the conduct of affairs at home, in the splendour and renown of his Court. He loved royal magnificence; he loved the arts with a taste formed by his beauty-loving mother, his young friends the Mancini sisters, one of whom had been his first love, and, above all, by the teaching and encouragement of that connoisseur the cardinal himself.

The year 1661, which had begun with Mazarin's death and ended with the birth of a dauphin, was a marvellous year in the reign of Louis XIV, for it saw the beginning of his enchantment with Versailles, and the moment when, for the first time, he fell over head and ears physically in love, with a passion that engaged his heart for the next six years.

22

LOUISE DE LA VALLIÈRE

 trangely enough it was the queen-mother who paved the way for her son's first passionate love affair. In her anxiety lest he make an unsuitable attachment she had hurried him into a loveless dynastic marriage with a princess he had never seen. She had hoped that love would follow or, at least, that he would settle down to family life with a young wife 'who would arouse his affection if not his desire'.

That, unhappily, was not to be. Marie Thérèse, as she was now called, was prepared to idolize her husband, but not go out of her way to please or amuse him. She was Spanish to the core, stiff and proud, in the way of all Spanish Infantas, and deeply religious, with the gloomy piety of the Escorial. Shocked by the frivolity of the French Court, she kept herself apart, making no effort to lose her foreign accent, and prepared to hate all things French, from the manners to the cooking. The Archbishop of Sens, who knew her well, described her thus: 'The queen was a saintly princess but lacked the social graces, being often disagreeable, and possessing none of the gentle arts that win a husband's heart. She too often displayed jealousy, and invariably failed to pay him those delicate compliments which kings are accustomed to receive from flattering courtiers. Her piety led her to go to church at times when the king desired her company in some party of pleasure, and she preferred to live retired among her dogs and Spanish dwarves rather than please him by taking part in the fêtes and other diversions with which he entertained his Court.'

For a time the king did his utmost to win her over, and at first they appeared happy enough; but she would not be coaxed and after a few months he gave up the attempt and sought livelier company. His behaviour to her was always impeccable. He slept in her bed, opened the ball with her whenever there was dancing, and partnered her in the first set. But he did not stay with her long and soon went off to join his boon companions.

Marie Thérèse has not been well treated by historians who tend to describe her as stupid, unco-operative and ill-educated. The truth now appears to be that she was better educated than is generally supposed and far from being unintelligent. But she was homesick for Spain and

23

for her father, and deeply disturbed by the love of pleasure and neglect of God that she thought she saw in her new country.

Nothing, indeed, could have been more different than the characters of her father, King Philip, and Louis XIV, her husband. The King of France was young, handsome and light-hearted. He loved beauty, high-spirits and fun, and favoured and rewarded those who combined gaiety and good looks with an appearance of happiness—'At the Court', said Saint-Simon, 'happy beauty was the finest dowry of all,' and the memoirist Primi Visconti, who spent ten years in Paris and at Versailles, reports that Cardinal Maldaccini exclaimed in delight, when he first saw the throng of laughing, smiling, chattering ladies and gentlemen of the Court, 'But this is just like a brothel!' That is as may be, but the fact remains that Louis XIV was regarded with genuine awe and respect. He was a superb actor of majesty, and there was something about him so imposing that wise men accustomed themselves to the sight of him before they risked speaking. He was meticulous in observing the laws of the Church in such matters as fasting and attending mass, but there was about him none of the holy gloom that put King Philip beyond the reach of his subjects.

The young queen made two fatal mistakes. In her displeasure at the French way of life, she refused to adapt herself, as Queen Anne had done, to the customs of her new country, or learn to ride and share the great pleasure her husband took in hunting. Worse, and to him unforgivable, she took her miseries and complaints to her mother-in-law for sympathy and support, which she received in good measure.

Queen Anne, though distressed, was not unduly alarmed at first. She saw her son's disappointment in his bride, but also his efforts to make a success of his marriage, and she did not believe that he would be unfaithful, especially when, in the early months of 1661, Marie Thérèse became pregnant. What she did not take into account was the irresistible charm of a newcomer to the Court, Charles I's youngest daughter, Henrietta of England, whose marriage to the king's brother, Philippe, Duc d'Orléans, had taken place in the spring. The beauty and charm of Henrietta are legendary in France. She was full of life and fun, an eager flirt, the possessor, according to Mme de Lafayette, of 'a pair of black eyes that burned with a flame so hot that no man could look into them without taking fire'. This she combined with a nature so simply warm and kind, so different from that of the proud French princesses, that everyone loved her.

The one man whom she could *not* persuade to love her was Monsieur, her husband; but no woman attracted him for he was given over to sodomy and, although he married twice and became the father of eleven children, four of whom lived to maturity, the begetting of

24

them was no pleasure to him. He had imagined himself in love with Henrietta in the flurry of excitement that attended their betrothal, but he very soon took against her, as he saw the courtiers focussing upon her the admiration which he felt to be his due.

For a time the king was captivated by Henrietta's sweetness and compelling charm. They flirted publicly in the ballroom and out hunting; Monsieur was furious, and Queen Anne took fright, for there were all the makings of a hideous scandal, and their behaviour in public

6. *A ball at the Louvre*

suggested a relationship which certainly could not be ascribed to
family affection. She spoke to them sternly and angrily in Monsieur's
presence, forcing them to reflect on the political consequences if they
persisted. This had the effect of bringing them to order; but Queen
Anne had little faith in the permanence of their reform, and set herself
to devise a most complicated scheme to divert the king's fancy.

She persuaded Henrietta to take into her household, as maids of
honour, three pretty young girls of no social standing who would
serve as companions for King Louis in his leisure hours, yet be
incapable of arousing his serious attention. Those she selected were
Mademoiselle de Pons, Mademoiselle de Chimerault, and Made-

moiselle de La Vallière. They were petted, given a most elegant and
becoming head-dress of heron's feathers, seated next to the king at
picnics, and invited to dance in his set at balls and in the ballets. Louis,
twenty-two years old and ready for love, eagerly embraced a new
freedom. He flirted outrageously with all three girls, which was
exactly what Queen Anne had intended, but gradually Louise de La
Vallière claimed all his attention, and the queen-mother saw with
dismay that he was falling in love again, but this time with an all-
absorbing, tender passion. It was the first great love affair of his life.

Louise, for her part, had been in love with him for years past, in the
way that all little girls blindly adore their heroes. Not for nothing had

she read the family motto, 'For the king, love undying as the altar-flame', which was carved on the chimney-piece of their country home. She was just seventeen years old when the king first noticed her, in June 1661, the daughter of a most gallant and unshakably loyal officer of the Touraine nobility whose family had been much impoverished by the wars. He had died six years earlier, and Louise's mother had taken a second husband, the Marquis de Saint-Remy, comptroller at Blois, of the household of the king's uncle, Gaston d'Orléans. This had brought the family within range of the Court; but when Louise was so unexpectedly appointed a maid of honour, they were still so poor that her mother was obliged to borrow the money for her Court dress.

As to Louise's beauty, opinions differed. One writer describes her as having a perfect complexion, curly fair hair, a kind smile, and eyes so tender yet so pure that they won, at first glance, the respect as well as the love of those who looked into them. He goes on to say that although by no means clever, she daily endeavoured to improve her mind with serious reading; that she had no ambition, held no views, and was more inclined to weave dreams about the king and their romantic love than to see him as he really was and strive to support him.

Another observer, Olivier Le Fèvre d'Ormesson, who a few months later chronicled the trial of Fouquet for corruption, was struck by her ugliness when he saw her at mass. 'Her eyes and complexion are certainly very good, but she is lean and hollow-cheeked, with an ugly mouth and teeth, and a bulbous nose in a face that is far too long. I must confess that I was surprised to find her so plain.' In the flattering portraits painted to please the king she does not appear plain, but her face suggests dreaminess and a lack of vital energy. Regarding her nature, however, there seems to have been general agreement—a sweet disposition, generous, retiring, kindly, but altogether too timid. Instead of taking pride in the position for which the king had chosen her, above all other women, she seemed ever-conscious of her failings and kept apologizing for them which, in the circumstances, appeared more than a little ridiculous, not to say irritating, to her fellow courtiers.

Why the king fell so wildly in love with her that he eagerly played Cophetua to her beggar-maid may perhaps be explained by the novelty that her gentle shyness represented. All his life, Louis XIV was inclined to be captivated by the charm of things new to him (which Saint-Simon considered a national failing), and certainly there was about Louise none of the bold assurance of the other Court ladies. He was extraordinarily moved by her sweet gentleness and apparent

28

fragility, combined with her magnificent physical courage and superb horsemanship. She was indeed a beautiful rider and quite without fear—'I saw her once in the Tuileries gardens', wrote an Italian priest who was on a visit to Paris, 'riding an Arab stallion, with only a silken cord for a bridle. As it cantered, she several times stood upright upon its back and then, with incomparable grace, sank down again;' and he went on to say that she had a Moorish groom who taught her many other daring feats of horsemanship.

Out hunting with the king, she was as bold as any man and rode as hard as he did; she was also an excellent shot, and able to hold her own with skilled swordsmen. Altogether, she was a perfect companion for him in his pleasures, fully sharing their dangers, yet so frail and delicate-seeming that she aroused all his protective instincts. One day, when they were walking alone together in the woods near Versailles, they encountered a violent storm, whereupon the king removed his own feathered hat, covered her golden curls, and thus, bareheaded, led her back to the château in the shelter of his protective arm. Such condescension was inconceivable; it was an occasion never to be forgotten by the courtiers who witnessed it.

At Fontainebleau, where the Court spent the first weeks of summer while Saint-Germain and the Tuileries were being cleaned and the 'bad air' dissipated, he wooed her ardently for a couple of weeks, after which their love was consummated in the bedroom of the Duc de Saint-Aignan, his first gentleman, and she became his acknowledged mistress. Fontainebleau was paradise for them, full of the memory of other royal lovers—Henri II and Diane de Poitiers, Henri IV and Gabrielle d'Estrées, whose intertwined initials remained painted on the ceilings and carved into the chimney-pieces.

In the daytime they rode or drove in the great forest, out of range of prying eyes, or walked together in the beautiful gardens, wilder and

9. Louise de La Vallière as Flora

10. Louis XIV as a young man

shadier than those of Saint-Germain. In the evening they picnicked by the lake with their young friends, gliding over the water in gondolas to the music of the twenty-four violins of the king's orchestra; then they danced, or watched ballets that told stories of gods and goddesses triumphant in their loves. Day by day their attachment grew; for both of them it was their first delirious experience of requited passion.

When the time came for the Court to leave Fontainebleau, the pretty little house at Versailles, so near to Saint-Germain, appeared the perfect setting for their love. The king established Louise there in his own suite, and hastened to be with her whenever he could be free from the work of governing France, a labour that came first with him and which he never shirked, not even for his beloved mistress. There were great sporting events at Versailles all through the summer, with tilting and jousting competitions, and many different trials of horsemanship. A small band of their close friends, with an average age of nineteen, were invited to take part, an élite who wore a much-coveted uniform of supreme elegance—a blue silk jacket, embroidered with silver lace, a scarlet waistcoat and, for the ladies, a most becoming hat trimmed with white feathers. 'These Amazons', said the Princesse de Condé, 'exceed everyone for smartness, and Mlle de La Vallière is the smartest of them all.' But the uniform was, in the king's mind, not merely a pleasure, a sop to the vanity of his chosen friends; it was a sign of a new order at the Court, the replacement (by a younger generation) of the old gentlemen and ladies who had set the tone in the time of his father.

Louise at this time was blissfully happy, living, she fondly believed, unnoticed by the outside world. Love in a cottage was her dream, and she waited for the man she adored, who so unfortunately was King of France, to come to her and gladly cast off his majesty, delighting in what she imagined to be the simple life. Mme de Sévigné's cousin, Bussy-Rabutin, explained the situation. 'It is undoubtedly true that La Vallière loved the king for himself alone. More than a year before he noticed her, she said many times to a certain lady, one of her closest friends, that she only wished he were of less exalted rank. It is generally believed that the teasing she received on that account reached the king's ears and made him curious to meet her. Then, since it is natural for generous hearts to return true love, he immediately fell in love with her. It was not her beauty that attracted him; he loved her for herself.'

Bussy-Rabutin said also of Louise: 'her love for him is so ardent that were he a mere country squire and she a great queen she would clearly be no less enchanted.' But Louise was not a great queen, only a very young girl of no social importance, too humble and too shy to enjoy the limelight, too religious not to be troubled by the sinfulness of adultery. Sometimes her great eyes filled with tears, which moved the king to caress and comfort her. He himself had no such qualms. Although he could see that his mother was deeply shocked by the attachment, the French people, as a whole, saw nothing very reprehensible in his having a mistress, or even bastard children. Several of the most noble families, the Vendômes, for example, had sprung from the illegitimate children of past kings, and it was generally considered that, having made a loveless marriage for the sake of France, the king deserved to seek love elsewhere, always provided that his mistress was unmarried and no husband made a cuckold.

Queen Anne did not share that view; she was fond of the unhappy queen who still loved her husband, and eventually she took the matter up with him. Louis's reply was to the effect that he did indeed feel religious scruples and sometimes a sense of sin; but that confession only confirmed him in his love for Louise. It was stronger than he, he could not fight against it and, moreover, he no longer felt the need to do so. As for Marie Thérèse, he was sorry for her unhappiness, would see that Louise treated her with profound respect, and do what he could to comfort her. Had he not held her hand, standing beside her bed the entire time of her protracted labour, feeding her himself with chicken broth from a gold spoon? History showed that the wives of kings came to accept such circumstances and understood the necessity. In the meantime, there was no reason why they should not all be happy.

11. Design by Le Brun for the Pyramide, one of the fountains in the gardens of Versailles

THE GREAT FÊTE AT VAUX-LE-VICOMTE

o one knows for certain when the idea came to Louis XIV of enlarging and beautifying the little house at Versailles. He loved magnificence and his taste for the arts had been encouraged and educated by Mazarin and his charming nieces. After Mazarin's death and the end of the *Frondes*, he needed to make his mark, and it is more than probable that the fête given in his honour by Nicolas Fouquet, the minister of finance, gave him the first inklings of what might be done to turn Versailles into an earthly paradise.

Fouquet was certainly corrupt, lining his pockets at the treasury's expense; but since he was lavish in spending and had close friends among the most powerful ladies at the Court, including Queen Anne, he could not be treated as of no consequence. After Mazarin's warning, on his deathbed, the king had shown a marked coldness to his finance minister, and had appointed Colbert to be his assistant so as to keep him under surveillance. Fouquet grew alarmed, and proceeded to attempt a return to favour by flattery and blandishment. He had built, at Vaux-le-Vicomte, a most magnificent palace with the finest gardens in Europe. He had engaged Le Vau as architect, Le Brun as decorator, and Le Nôtre to design the landscape. He also engaged Molière and La Fontaine to sing its praises. He could not have chosen better.

When the time came for a grand opening, Fouquet gave a party of unimaginable splendour and invited the king. It was a fatal move; but he, like many others, totally misunderstood the character of Louis XIV, believing that his interest in statecraft was a mere whim, and that in a few months' time he would return to sports and dancing, leaving the government and supreme power in the hands of a first minister who would share his lavish tastes. It was a misconception that precipitated his ruin.

The king had known for some time of the building of Vaux (it had taken no more than five years to complete), and he had approved of the idea of a great house designed, built and decorated by Frenchmen; with a garden laid out according to the plans of a French gardener, and tapestries designed and woven, not in Italy, but in factories on the estate. He had already, on two or three occasions, visited Vaux to

12 & 13. Nicolas Fouquet,
minister of finance, with
opposite a view of the gardens at
Vaux-le-Vicomte

inspect the work in progress, but nothing had prepared him for the outrageous magnificence of the finished product.

At three o'clock on 17 August 1661 he left Fontainebleau. Arriving at the château at six, he entered the beautiful wrought-iron gates, with their gold paint flashing in the sunlight of a perfect summer evening, and, driving through lawns adorned with statues of Greek gods and goddesses (all of them the work of French sculptors), past a charming orangery, drew up at the door of the vast palace, crowned with a central dome, and with a frontage of more than seventy yards.

Fouquet was at the great door to do the honours, showing the king room after room hung with tapestries, their ceilings painted by Le Brun, full of exquisitely beautiful furniture and rare carpets from Persia and China, amid a wealth of the sweet-smelling flowers which King Louis so much loved. There was displayed a kind of luxury that was new to him and far beyond his own means, and Fouquet, escorting him, underlined the insult by offering to present his sovereign with whatever he most admired.

Later, when night had fallen, they went into the garden, a fairyland of cascades and fountains illuminated by torchlight. Supper was served to the music of violins conducted by Lulli, and afterwards Molière's troupe of actors performed *Les Fâcheux* (The Bores) a *comédie-ballet* specially composed for the occasion by Molière himself. The open-air theatre was backed by a wide pool, and at first Molière appeared alone, apparently in despair, crying out that his actors had deserted him, and imploring the king to use his magical power to

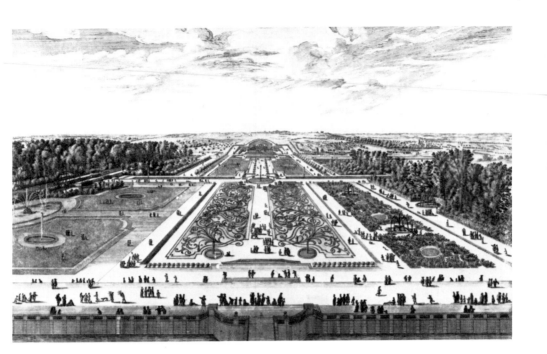

work a miracle. The king then made a gesture, and at once a huge shell came floating across the water, unfolding to disclose a nymph who ordered the surrounding statues to come to life and the trees to burst into song, whereupon fawns and satyrs rushed upon the stage in a wild dance with heroes and goddesses of ancient Greece.

After the play, the château and gardens were lit with hundreds of lanterns. A boat in the shape of a whale moved slowly along the central canal firing burst after burst of rockets, while trumpets and kettledrums made the sounds of a battle between fire and water. In a grand finale so many rockets were let off over the wide path back to the château that the king, on his way to *media noce* (the midnight feast), appeared to walk beneath a canopy of fire.

The colossal pride of Louis XIV, something which Fouquet had not taken into account, was profoundly insulted. He was, like all his courtiers, overcome by the beauty of Vaux and the splendour of the fête; but to him Fouquet appeared not as a generous host and future collaborator, but as a self-evident thief who had enriched himself from the treasury over the years when his king was hard pressed to find money for the country's essential needs.

He had said nothing to Fouquet at the time; but was heard to whisper to his mother as they gazed at a palace that far outshone in splendour the royal residences of France, 'Ah! Madame, should we not make these people disgorge?' That was perhaps the moment when he decided to make an example of Fouquet and transform Versailles.

But he acted with restraint. Fouquet was not a nobody who might be swept away unnoticed; he had powerful allies in the Parlement and among the nobility, and his sudden disgrace might cause unrest, possibly even a renewal of the *Frondes*. It was therefore not until nineteen days after the famous fête that the arrest was made; a trial followed that lasted three years, and Fouquet, found guilty of treason and corruption, was sent for life to the desolate fortress of Pignerol, far away on the border of Italy. As they led him away he was heard to exclaim, 'They make a bad mistake. I had made my pile and was just about to make theirs.'

Having disposed of the villain, the king took into his own service the team of artists that had created the wonders of Vaux. The château itself was left to Mme Fouquet so that she might repay her husband's debts and part of the huge sums he had embezzled; the contents the king took for his personal share. The pictures and ornaments were put in store at Saint-Germain, while the curtains, some of them made of cloth of gold, and the beautiful tapestries went back to the work-shops* to have the Fouquet arms replaced by the lilies of France. Among the treasures particularly prized by King Louis were the thousand orange trees, worth a fortune in themselves, that he had greatly admired in Fouquet's orangery.

Another effect of that unforgettable evening seems to have been to fix in the king's mind the desire to leave Paris, 'where there is nowhere to walk,' and take up permanent residence in the country. Saint-Simon says in his *Mémoires* that 'he conceived the idea that the people would hold him in greater veneration if he avoided the rabble and were not every day to be seen.'

His first idea was to settle at Saint-Germain and in the following years he gave fêtes and other entertainments there, in order to draw the social world away from Paris to savour the pleasures of a country life. But his heart was not at Saint-Germain; it was with the pretty, shy and artless girl with whom he was madly in love and who lived at Versailles, that had seemed to them a perfect place in which to hide their attachment. Louis himself had taken a great fancy to the little house; Colbert said that he was 'taken with the idea of smartening it up, making it fit for royal persons to enjoy there the seasonal pleasures.' The Court spent a week there in the summer of 1663 and saw four plays acted by Molière's company, including one, entitled *L'Impromptu de Versailles*, written especially for the occasion.

Vaux had given the king a vision of what Versailles might become, for he seems to have decided to leave as his monument, not the restoration of some great historic building, such as the Louvre or

*Colbert later moved Fouquet's workshop at Maincy, near Vaux, to Paris, and established the great tapestry factory 'Les Gobelins'.

14. *The Grand Cascade at Vaux-le-Vicomte*

Saint-Germain, but the creation of something of incomparable beauty in a place where, before his time, the world had seen nothing but emptiness and desolation.

Already he was buying large tracts of land in the neighbourhood, including one parcel of fifteen hundred acres that went to make the small park, for the race-course and the sporting events that Louise delighted in. Le Vau was set to draw plans for the enlargement of the little château, with the seemingly impossible instruction that nothing was to be changed. They both thought it perfection—'If you pull it down', said Louis to Le Vau, 'I shall build it up again brick by brick.' In the meantime, he was allowed to build for Louise a charming dairy, an orangery to house the thousand orange trees taken from Fouquet, and, at a sufficient distance from the house to make a pleasant stroll, a menagerie for rare birds and animals—including an elephant and a camel—to amuse visitors and serve as models for painters and decorators.

16. *Camels, sketched by Le Brun*

15. *The menagerie at Versailles*

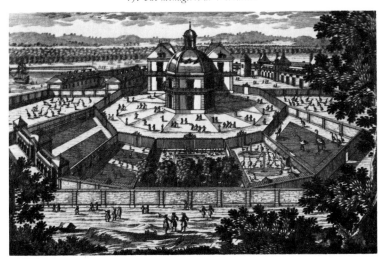

17. André Le Nôtre

18. The palace and gardens of Versailles in 1668

The king was enchanted by this particular building: he pored over the plans, plaguing Le Vau with innumerable questions regarding the fountains and the supply of water for them. Water, as it turned out, was to be an almost insuperable problem on a terrain where there was no running water and neither lakes nor rivers to be tapped in the immediate neighbourhood. New and larger pumps had recently been set up to draw the water of nearby village ponds and, as a distraction, Le Vau had placed the entire system of taps and levers on the balcony

of the menagerie, so that the king could himself control the flow, making the jets rise and fall as he pleased, and getting exceedingly wet in the process.

In the gardens work proceeded apace. Le Nôtre, just back from England where he had designed the garden at Greenwich for Charles II, was preparing a very different treatment for the swampy, treeless land about Versailles. His grand geometric design was immediately established and never altered. He showed every plan and drawing to the king, who initialled them; and every few days took him on a personally conducted tour to gain his consent and hear his comments. As he spoke of tall trees giving a third dimension to a flat landscape, and described bands of dark yew trees forming a background to two big stretches of water adorned with statues that would lighten and bring relief to a wide terrace before the château; as he told of the great double flight of steps that would guide the eye to the horizon; of a central pathway crossing a green carpet three hundred yards long, to be edged with white statues, and dark groves leading to a most magnificent fountain to be named 'the basin of Apollo', behind which would sparkle the waters of the grand central canal, the king went into ecstasies. 'Oh! Le Nôtre,' he exclaimed, 'You shall have five thousand livres for each of these ideas!' Whereat, after several repetitions of that promise, Le Nôtre stopped and looked at him — 'Sire,' he said, 'I dare not go on, you will be ruined.'

Louis XIV delighted in Le Nôtre. He probably liked him better than any of his courtiers, and there grew up between them a relationship of almost filial and paternal affection. No detail was too small for the king's attention; he loved to work on those last touches in which, he believed, perfection lay; he was enthralled by his vision of a beauty and majesty that would make his Court world-famous, and he loved Le Nôtre for his genius and understanding. He himself worked on the plans and drawings, for in the Bibliothèque Nationale, in Paris, there is one such, with a note in Le Nôtre's handwriting: 'This is the king's own design, carried out by his gardener André Le Nôtre.' Had he been willing to accept honours and ennoblement, the king would have heaped rewards upon him; but the great man refused everything except, for the sake of convenience, permission to build himself a little house in the grounds of Versailles, and another in the Tuileries gardens where he was still superintendent. Ennoblement he had no wish for. 'What should I do with a coat of arms, Sire? I have one already—two slugs rampant on a cabbage leaf.'

Time was now of the first importance. The Versailles gardens must be made immediately and the glories of those at Vaux wiped from people's memories; above all, there must soon be a fête of unsurpassed beauty and pleasure to honour Louise. A whole army of labourers was therefore transported from Vaux to dig the bed of the great canal and the pools and basins around the fountains. Tall forest trees were dug up and moved on huge carts to be replanted in the new gardens; many died in transit, as was unavoidable, but others were brought to fill their places.

There were casualties among the labourers and the king paid compensation—thirty livres for a broken arm or leg, sixty for the loss of an eye, a hundred to the widows of men who fell from scaffoldings or were crushed by falling trees. But there were conditions attached. No complaints or rancour were allowed, and one poor woman who railed against the king when her son fell to his death was promptly arrested. She was ordered to cease in her abuse, and when she still persisted she was publicly whipped at the king's express command.

Every aspect of the great work fascinated the king; not only the making of plans, but the art of planting and pruning shrubs and fruit trees in his new kitchen garden, a skill he learned under the eye of the famous botanist Jean de La Quintinie, whom he made superintendent. Gardening gave him enormous satisfaction, and confirmed his belief in the paternal nature of absolute monarchy, for La Quintinie taught him that plants needed and responded to personal attention. 'Plant your Bon-Chrétien pears near the house', he said, 'where they catch the master's eye each day. Human breath is very agreeable to them.' The king loved to see his trees and flowers looking well and happy in places which he himself had chosen for them. They repaid him by thriving and if they wilted despite all his care they could be thrown away without fuss or protest. If only his people could be treated in the same way; if only they would trust and obey him he would do wonders for them; for he thought he genuinely cared for his subjects and, provided they did not obstruct his wishes or hamper him in his pleasures, loved to see them happy. But they seemed to be forever making demands or protests; moreover, when he dismissed or exiled offenders there was always such a fuss.

One man who perpetually made a fuss, without risking dismissal, was Colbert, the new minister of finance. He foresaw that Louis XIV's passion for Versailles, 'that most thankless of sites', would become insatiable, and thought him mad to spend millions on its development. He protested vigorously; daring to reproach the king for 'neglecting the Louvre, which is beyond all doubt the world's most splendid palace . . . The house at Versailles', he said, 'is for Your Majesty's pleasure, not a fit monument for your glory,' and he ended by appealing to the king's pride:

'Your Majesty is well aware that apart from victory in battle, nothing better betokens the grandeur and fame of princes than the buildings they leave to posterity. Princes are judged by the palaces that they build in their lifetimes. How tragic it would be were the greatest king, the most virtuous of princes, to be judged on the merits of Versailles.'

The king trusted Colbert and almost invariably followed his advice; but he remained unconvinced by these particular arguments. He foresaw not only the glory and fame attaching to his dream, but the

19. The building of Versailles

revival of French industry in the realization of it. The silk-mills of Tours and Lyons had come almost to a standstill in recent years; the metal-workers and glass-blowers, the goldsmiths and tapestry-makers had been out of work. They would now be needed not only for Versailles but for the houses of wealthy noblemen eager to follow the fashion. Money was not then a problem, for France was not at war, and Colbert, since Fouquet's departure, had been bringing order to the finances. Checks were now being made on every payment from the royal treasury, not only by the minister but by the king himself. 'His Majesty', wrote Colbert, 'sees or hears of every expense, and considers it at least six times before consenting to make the payment legal.' There was no longer any deficit in the State accounts, but on the contrary a rising surplus.

Louis XIV's reply to Colbert's protests was to make him minister of works and buildings, with instructions to arrange, for the following spring, a fête at Versailles so magnificent that the one at Vaux would be entirely eclipsed.

PLEASURES OF THE ENCHANTED ISLE

y September 1663, Louis XIV decided that the Versailles gardens had reached such a state of perfection that they might be shown to the world. Le Nôtre and his vast army had been operating for no more than two years; but their progress had been incredibly fast. The grand design was not yet completed (it never was); but the main lines were already there, the huge stretches of water shone in the sunlight, there were masses of tall trees where none had been before, and the 'green carpet' lay flawless between the lines of statues and the dark hedge of yews that led down to the Apollo fountain. Outside the orangery, the precious orange trees in their white tubs were a beautiful sight, and on the wide terrace before the château all the fountains played.

The king issued invitations to the entire Court for a week-long festival to be held in the gardens and park of Versailles, opening on 7 May of the following year. It was to be entitled *Les Plaisirs de l'Ile Enchantée*, and Queen Anne was to be the guest of honour. No one doubted, however, that the real queen of the revels would be Louise de La Vallière, or that the king's intention was to make known his love for her. The courtiers were not wholly delighted, for work on the little château was far from being finished and there was no prospect of anyone being given a lodging. 'All the courtiers are furious,' said Mme de Sévigné, 'the Duc de Guise and the Duc d'Elbeuf will have nowhere to shelter if it rains.' But Mme de Sévigné had personal reasons for grumbling; Fouquet had been her friend, and she was little inclined to praise Versailles.

Preparations during the winter proceeded at great speed. Carlo Vigarani, a famous Italian stage designer, whom Mazarin had summoned from Italy, was already at work creating the mechanical effects that were so much admired in the seventeenth-century ballets—chariots descending from Heaven laden with gods and goddesses, thunderstorms, earthquakes, battles and shipwrecks appearing as though by magic and vanishing in a puff of smoke.

Many of these effects were left to the last moment, many were clumsily contrived, but the beauty of the gardens was a revelation to the courtiers, and as night fell, a blaze of light from thousands of torches and tens of thousands of candles fixed on the trees and bushes turned the scene to fairyland.

In the interior of the château, parts of which were for the first time shown to the public, the drawing-rooms had been redecorated and newly furnished with the treasures from Vaux. Queen Anne was enchanted by the bright colours, the shining gold paint and marble pillars, and the profusion of flowers in vases everywhere. She admired especially the huge tubs of jasmine that filled the house with a delicious scent, unfamiliar at that time to fashionable noses.

Out of doors, as the light faded, the fête became truly magnificent, for the courtiers wore their very best, and the torchlight brought out the richness of the ladies' silk dresses and the gold lace and diamonds on the men's velvet coats. The audience took their seats in the open-air theatre for the first night's entertainment, an arrangement of part of Ariosto's epic-poem *Orlando Furioso*, describing the sojourn of brave Rogero and several other valiant knights in the island palace of the wicked enchantress Alcina, who had the power to change her lovers into trees or beasts or fountains when she had done with them.

It opened with a fanfare of trumpets and a torchlight procession headed by the king in the rôle of Rogero. He was a splendid sight, riding with ease and grace a beautiful charger caparisoned in flame-coloured velvet, with golden harness that sparkled with rubies and diamonds. 'His kingly bearing', wrote an observer, 'set him far above the stature of ordinary mortals.' He was followed by a page bearing a shield on which shone the device of a sun in splendour, and the motto, 'I neither rest nor turn aside.' This was the first time that the sun was used to symbolize the radiance and glory of Louis XIV.

Those taking part in the play that followed formed the remainder of the procession; nobles, professional actors, dancers, all mixed up together, with Molière's troupe among them, dressed as the signs of the Zodiac and the four seasons. Then came animals from the king's menagerie, representing countries of the far east, and last of all the

20. Horsemen led by the king at a display in the Place du Carrousel, 1662

chariot of Apollo, glittering gold, and surrounded by a throng of dancers in exotic costumes.

Then the play began. It showed Rogero and his knights held captive for many months on Alcina's enchanted isle, entranced by her beauty and the delights of carnal pleasure. He might never have escaped, had not a magic ring that destroyed the spell been given to him. As he turned it on his finger, the wicked Alcina, her island palace and the lake surrounding it vanished in a sheet of flame, and a display of fireworks such as had never before been seen. The height and number of the rockets were said to have formed a spectacle so magnificent as to make it appear that Heaven and earth and all the water round the magic isle were turned to fire.

The second night saw the performance of a play, *La Princesse d'Élide*, composed for the occasion by Molière at the special request of the king who wished to celebrate his love for Louise and her position as his official mistress. As usual, what the king wished for he wished to have at once, and poor Molière was given no time to develop his ideas. So hard-pressed was he that he was forced to hand the play over unfinished, with the last act still in prose. That was not considered a great matter; for in the king's eyes Molière had done his work, there being many references to love's young dream and the art of courtly love. The play ended with a tribute to glory, won not on the battlefield but in the war of love. 'Some weaknesses', said Molière, 'are far from being shameful; they should rather be extolled as providing life's most glorious moments.'

The struggle for ascendancy in love was a popular theme at that period. Shakespeare had used it in *Much Ado about Nothing*, *As You Like It* and *A Midsummer Night's Dream*, but with more success; Molière's ideas seem to have been cramped by the need to remember the occasion and keep within the bounds of courtly propriety. *La Princesse d'Élide* was not his happiest effort.

That day was the first of the five-day tournament, with tilting

matches in which the king took part. Quite unexpectedly, Louise's brother won a prize, and she was proud and delighted when Queen Anne presented him with a fine sword in a gold scabbard encrusted with diamonds. Every evening, while the fête lasted, there were concerts by Lulli's orchestra, and out-of-door suppers like the one at Vaux. Four thousand candles shed light on the tables, and delicious meals were served by fauns and wood-nymphs. Later there were firework displays and ballets in which the king and Louise danced with many of the courtiers.

The festival was generally declared to have been a magnificent success, far better even than the one at Vaux which, as the king had hoped, was fading from people's memories. There were several noteworthy converts; La Fontaine, for instance, who had been Fouquet's friend, and ecstatic on the subject of Vaux, now wrote: 'Everyone will have heard of the marvels produced at this latest festival—the palaces transformed into gardens, the gardens changed back to palaces. The astonishing speed with which these wonders were performed will make people believe in magic.'

The courtiers, especially the two queens, seated in the front row of the audience, appear to have been delighted to see the plays and ballets, and admire the king's horsemanship in the tourneys and tilting competitions. Everyone, with one exception, was in raptures, but the girl whom the king loved, and who was the real queen of the revels, sat blushing, uncomfortable, and very near to tears. People turned to look enviously at her, and turned away disappointed and slightly contemptuous, finding her inadequate, unable to enjoy her moment of glory.

Poor Louise felt their scorn, and it made her ashamed; but glory meant nothing to her, and the king's resolve to enlarge Versailles and give her a high position at the Court shocked her and filled her with terror. She adored him, but stubbornly insisted on his taking her on her own terms, in privacy, living the simple life, as it had been in the first days. He was still in love with her, but he was beginning to love glory more, and felt the urge to rouse her to share his dream of splendour. Louise, however, would not be moved, and he found her tears and bashfulness increasingly wearisome.

For a time his fancy lighted on the Princesse de Monaco, a very pretty girl, not at all averse to love, and surrounded by a multitude of admirers. When the rumour got about that the king had 'noticed her',

22. Louis XIV as Apollo

there was an explosion of jealousy, and someone sent Louise an anonymous letter in the belief that she would make a scene and cause a rupture. That, however, was not in Louise's nature. Sure of the king's love and herself incapable of jealousy, she simply handed him the letter, without comment or complaint, showing the kind of trust that always moved him deeply. He soon guessed that the writer was his old friend the Duc de Villeroy and, summoning him for an interview, extracted a confession, after which he, perhaps rather surprisingly, forgave him. It was, however, characteristic of Louis XIV to be steadfastly loyal to the friends of his boyhood. What he would put up with from no one were grudges, miseries and glum faces; they were frequently the reason for peremptory dismissals from the Court.

Louise no doubt was distressed; but she comforted herself with the joyful notion that she had at last found a friend at the Court who sympathized, encouraged, and gave her confidence. Strangely enough this lady belonged to the smart set, the very people whose scorn and malice most intimidated Louise. Her name was Françoise de Montespan—Athénaïs, as she chose to be called—just twenty-three years old, the wife of a wild young Gascon, and by birth a Mortemart, one of the oldest families of France.

There could not be imagined a greater contrast to the gentle, retiring Louise than this audacious beauty. Mme de Sévigné called them the dew and the torrent, for whereas Louise was silent and sweet-

23. The first day of the Pleasures of the Enchanted Isle. The procession of the king

24. *The third day of the* Pleasures of the Enchanted Isle. *The firework display*

natured, Françoise, as she was then called, was voluble, voluptuous, sparkling with witty talk that kept those around her in gales of laughter and was rarely untinged with malice. There was never a dull moment when she was in the company, and Louise, well aware of her own shortcomings, welcomed her to enliven the king's daily visits to the Hôtel Brion, the little house at Versailles which he had recently given her. She came to believe that she could not do without Mme de Montespan's support, and they were virtually inseparable. It does not seem to have occurred to her that Françoise might have been using her to gain intimacy with the king; but however that may have been, there was no apparent cause for jealousy, since the king quite clearly disliked her. He was heard to say to his brother, 'She is trying to start a flirtation; but she does not appeal to me.'

Perhaps the king did not wish to be charmed. The fact that Françoise was married may have deterred him, for Queen Anne would have been horrified by the thought of a doubly adulterous attachment, and she had so ground into her son the fear of God that he would not lightly have set aside the prospect of eternal damnation. Moreover, he still loved Louise: although the idyllic charm of their first passion had abated he loved her tenderly and did not wish to hurt her.

Françoise de Montespan was in no hurry. She was prepared to wait, for she was consumed by ambition and rightly conceived that her

49

moment would come in the future when the king's plans for glory had matured. He himself was at that time disinclined for love. Obsessed by his passion for Versailles and his friendship with his gardeners, he went nearly every day to work physically among his trees and plants. There was plenty still to do, wide tracts of land remained to be cleared, swamps required draining, and water, the biggest problem of all, had to be brought in abundance from every pond and stream in the district. An aqueduct was already constructed, and all over the Satory plain, where army manoeuvres were held, tall windmills turned, emptying a vast number of newly-dug wells. Yet all these resources were proving insufficient even for the needs of the fourteen hundred fountains already functioning, and provided a mere trickle compared with the great flow required for future developments.

The army of labourers taken from Vaux-le-Vicomte was still busily employed planting forests of the great trees transported to Versailles. The park had taken shape, and, although Le Vau's plan for the little château was not yet observable, the main lines had begun to appear. An Italian traveller, writing home, was overcome with admiration. 'Considering the appearance of the buildings, the abundance of game for hunting, the luxuries and pleasures, Versailles will exceed all the king's other residences, not excluding Fontainebleau. Three high-roads to Paris are already in use, and will gradually be improved. They cover twenty-one miles and are set between a double line of trees. There are to be three tracks; the paved central way for coaches will be twenty-five yards wide, and two tracks, one on either side, will be raised to form dykes. All of this will cost the king an immense fortune, for the district is hilly, and the gradients must be levelled over a distance of seven miles. Yet if these roads are ever finished, they will be acclaimed as the finest in the world.'

The cost was indeed enormous, and Colbert continued to protest. 'Should Your Majesty seek to trace', he wrote on 28 September 1665, 'the whereabouts in Versailles of the 500,000 écus spent there in the past two years, you would have great difficulty in discovering them.' But the king was not to be diverted. Versailles and not the Louvre was to be the seat of his power, a witness to the glory of his reign, the length of which he seems never to have doubted. His affection for the place itself; his joy in the plans of his gardener and his architect; the general admiration; the immense success of the fêtes, filled him with the urge to continue against all opposition. He believed that he was creating out of nothing a masterpiece for posterity, and who shall say that he was wrong?

26. The siege of Lille

27. The siege of Tournai

MME DE MONTESPAN
ATTRACTS NOTICE

ueen Anne, whose health had been failing during the past year, fell ill with cancer of the breast during the summer of 1665, and died in agony the following January. The king, who loved his mother and was deeply distressed by her pain, had his bed moved into her room during the closing stages until, on the night of her death, he was overcome with grief and the doctors carried him away. The person with most cause to mourn Queen Anne's death was poor Marie Thérèse, for she lost the one person who was fond of her, her steadfast friend and confidante in a strange land where she was universally despised and disliked. Poor young queen, it was her tragedy that she continued to be in love with the king who, although he treated her always with studied courtesy, publicly insulted her by open and continued unfaithfulness.

The king's grief was intense, but not long-lasting. It was not in his nature to harbour sorrow; indeed, he made it his policy, even his duty (and that of his courtiers) to be cheerful at all times. Life at the Court of France must go on, and personal affliction never be allowed to mar the atmosphere of social well-being. Many years later, on the evening after the sudden death of his brother Philippe Duc d'Orléans, he had the drawing-room at Marly set with card-tables, with the orchestra playing as usual. 'He has bidden me play cards tonight,' said his grandson the Duc de Bourgogne, 'he will have no one bored at Marly.'

It was perhaps only natural that when his sorrow had subsided, the king should have felt relief. He was now free from his mother's strict surveillance, her reproaches for any neglect of religious observances and her shocked disapproval of his love affairs. He was no longer a boy, but a grown man, young, strong, and twenty-eight years old, fully capable, in his own estimation, of supervising his own conduct. During his mother's illness, he had held a little in check the activities at Versailles because they disquieted her, but now he could give them free rein. France was again at war, protecting Marie Thérèse's right to the Spanish succession in the Netherlands. The French armies were victorious and industry prosperous. No need now to heed Colbert.

The army of labourers working at Versailles was increased to thirty thousand, and Louis XIV was constantly among them, urging more

speed, inspecting every detail. The word went out that the king must
be obeyed and obeyed instantly. To please him everything had to be
done in a hurry, and poor Colbert, now minister of works as well as of
war, told his son, who acted as his assistant, that one of them, at least,
must be on the site at five in the morning to ensure that each portion of
the work was completed in the time which the king had set.

Poor Colbert! Despite all his zeal, he failed to satisfy. Some of the
new walls had begun to crumble, due to faulty workmanship, and the
king held him personally responsible. He felt the injustice so deeply
that he retired to bed.

Meanwhile both the queen and Louise had become pregnant,
Louise for the third time; her two other children by the king had died
in infancy. This baby, a daughter, was born in October 1667, and in
the following January the queen also gave birth to a daughter. The
king, who found pregnant women a great bore, seems to have been
very little interested in the additions to his family, or in the queen's
confinement. He was seen less than two weeks later laughing with
Louise at a particularly funny farce by Molière, and a ballet with the
Italian players, a troupe of comedians often in trouble for their
bawdiness. There were several grand fêtes at Versailles that summer;
Louise was the centre of them all, and enjoyed the king's undivided

attention. None the less the clouds were gathering. 'In the midst of all the pleasures,' wrote the Prince de Condé, 'the ladies are busy mischief-making. What chiefly riles them is their extreme jealousy of Mlle de La Vallière. There are not many who do not regard her with intense envy.'

Yet when Louise was again pregnant in the following spring, the king insisted on her staying at home, instead of accompanying the queen and her ladies (including Mme de Montespan), whom he took to amuse him at the army's headquarters on the Dutch border. Before leaving, he rewarded Louise by making her a duchess and legitimating their baby daughter, giving her the names Marie Anne de Bourbon. Several advantages and greatly enhanced dignity accompanied the title. Duchesses, for example, might leave their coaches in the forecourts of the royal palaces, and have them lined with scarlet cloth, although it must hang loose and not be nailed into place. That suggestion of permanence was allowed only to princes and princesses of the royal blood. Duchesses, moreover, wore trains three yards long, and had the right to a tabouret, a folding stool on which they sat in the queen's presence while the rest of the Court remained standing—a coveted and most convincing sign of their superiority.

Louis XIV may have wished to honour Louise, and give her confidence during his absence; but to Louise herself the advancement

29. The Duchesse de Montpensier, la Grande Mademoiselle

30. The entry of Louis XIV and the queen into Douai, 1667

brought no satisfaction. She said it was like the reward given to retiring servants—what is known today as a 'golden handshake'—and, indeed, a rumour was going about that when the king told the queen of his intention to honour Louise, he had given his solemn promise never again to make love to her. He would appear to have been growing tired of her, and not averse to the idea of seeking love and friendship elsewhere. Her frequent tears no longer moved him; she no longer cheered him, and from her his darling plans for the glory of Versailles evoked no response. He was still fond of her and cared for her well-being; but when she laid the blame for his diminishing ardour upon the queen and, disobeying his orders, forced herself upon the royal party on their way to the army, she effectively destroyed her remaining charm in his eyes. It was an occasion which horrified the court, and La Grande Mademoiselle* tells what happened.

'On the second night of the excursion, when the queen had reached La Fère, I observed that her ladies were acting strangely and talking in hushed voices. They were sitting on their trunks in the corridor, saying that they were tired and unable to sleep because the queen had been prostrated by the news that the Duchesse de La Vallière was on

*Court name for Anne-Marie-Louise d'Orléans, Duchesse de Montpensier, the daughter of Gaston d'Orléans, Louis XIII's brother.

her way to join them. When I entered the bedroom, I found the queen in tears and too weak to move. Mme de Montausier, her lady-in-waiting, was shrugging her shoulders and saying over and over again, "You see the condition to which Her Majesty is reduced." Mme de Montespan, who was also present, was loud in her cries, exclaiming that the queen was much to be pitied, for her fears were only too well-founded.'

Louise's stubborn streak was making itself apparent. Next morning she arrived just as the royal party were about to leave, and although the queen had ordered the outer door to be barred against her she managed to get in by the back way, climb the stairs, and confront Her Majesty. The queen would not speak to her and, moreover, issued orders that no food or refreshment was to be given her.

'The talk in the royal coach that morning', continued Mlle de Montpensier, 'was all of the Duchesse de La Vallière, Mme de Montespan declaring that she wondered at her courage in daring to face the queen's wrath: "Evidently", she said, "the king had not given her leave to come, and she must have known before she started that he would be very angry and that Her Majesty would not receive her . . . Heaven preserve me", she concluded, "from ever being the king's mistress. Were I to suffer that mischance, I should spend my life in hiding."'

Marie Thérèse gave orders before retiring that none of her ladies were to leave next morning before she, herself, was on the road; but Louise, waking early, defied her and, calling for her carriage, set out across country at top speed, so as to be the first lady to join the king. When, later in the day, he rode up to the door of the queen's coach and heard his wife's bitter complaints, he went immediately to Louise, who was not seen again on that excursion.

No one appeared more shocked by the new duchess's conduct than Mme de Montespan, or more distressed at the queen's embarrassment. Realizing that Louise had had her day, she set herself to establishing a firm base from which to climb, and began by insinuating herself into the queen's confidence and favour. The method she employed was to outdo poor Marie Thérèse in piety, showing a positive addiction for fasting and church services, and being seen to take Communion at least once a week. She was also exceptionally witty and amusing, and every night at the queen's *coucher*, when the king joined the ladies, she kept them in fits of laughter, describing the men who tried to make love to her in her husband's absence and the tricks she played on them. All of this had a double purpose, to give the queen proof of her good morals, and show the king that she was heart-free. It was at this time that she dropped the name Françoise and asked to be called Athénaïs, a name she had adopted on her marriage. It sounded more fashionable, in the classical vein then so much in vogue, and certainly better suited to the illustrious future which she had in mind.

At Avesnes, on the Dutch border, where the royal party spent the remainder of the summer, it was first observed that Athénaïs had attracted the king's notice. They were all lodged in a large house belonging to Mme de Montausier, the queen's first lady-in-waiting. Their bedrooms were on the first floor, and a gentleman trooper of the King's Musketeers stood on guard every night before the king's door. That keen observer Mlle de Montpensier noted that before very long this sentry had been shifted to the ground floor, and that the king had become quite amazingly cheerful. 'One day at dinner,' she wrote, 'I heard the queen complain that he had not come to bed until after four o'clock, when it was almost daylight. "I cannot imagine", she said, "what he can have been doing." The king, who overheard her, protested that he had worked far into the night, reading dispatches and writing replies; but as he spoke, he turned away so that no one should see his smile. As for me,' concluded Mademoiselle, 'I kept my eyes in my lap, and took particular care not to meet his gaze.'

It was becoming plain that the king had fallen in love with Mme de Montespan with a passion very different from his tender, romantic devotion to Louise de La Vallière, for never were two women more complete contrasts. Athénaïs had none of the sweet gentleness that caused people to compare Louise to a modest violet. She was, on the contrary, full of vital energy, ambitious, cruel, triumphant, with a loveliness that made people compare her to an opening rose. There can be no doubt of her great beauty. Even when she was ten years older, Mme de Sévigné tells us she was dazzling, for she had a radiance, a sparkle, that brought life and fun and laughter wherever she went. The secret of her enormous charm lay in her conversation, her irresistibly humorous way of talking, the particular gift of the Mortemart family which at that time consisted of the duke her father, herself, her elder sister Mme de Thiange, her younger sister, who became the Abbess of Fontévrault in 1670, and their brother the Duc de Vivonne born in 1636. Voltaire said of them: 'Those five persons enchanted everyone by their conversation, an inimitable turn of phrase, a mixture of jokes, pretended innocence and art.'

Saint-Simon, after declaring that the wit of the Mortemarts was indescribable, proceeded to describe it vividly in his portrait of Mme de Castries, Athénaïs's niece: 'Mme de Castries knew everything— history, philosophy, mathematics, the dead languages, yet she never appeared to know more than how to speak good French, which she did with eloquence, grace, and wit, even on the dullest subjects, and

with that inimitable turn of phrase which only the Mortemarts possess. Pleasant, amusing, grave, or gay, she was all things to all men, captivating when she sought to please, genuinely funny, brilliantly witty, and delivering her sallies in a manner that made them unforgettable. She was captious, liable to be horrified by a thousand things in a plaintive tone that brought the house down. When she chose she could be cruelly cutting; but she was a good friend, kind and courteous, always ready to assist; not a coquette but responsive to the charms of others when she found them to her liking.' Saint-Simon gives us perhaps an important clue, when he continues that she was like a *biscuit manqué*, a flat and very innocent-looking sponge cake that unexpectedly contained a most potent measure of rum.

The king delighted in Mme de Montespan's conversation which reminded him of his boyhood and the witty talk in his mother's drawing-room. He began to take her in the royal coach on all his journeys. When they returned to Saint-Germain after a triumphant campaign that saw the capture of Douai, Tournai and Lille, the Duke of Savoy's envoy reported having watched the king chatting with Mme de Montespan before leaving, and seen her step into the royal coach. 'The king sat beside the queen on the back seat; placed the other lady next to him by the coach-door and talked exclusively to her

throughout the entire journey. What is amusing is that the queen does
not suspect an "affair", and is encouraged by him to be jealous of La
Vallière.'

Louise herself did not at first attribute the change in the king to
Mme de Montespan, and continued to regard the queen as her enemy.
It says much for her good nature that even after learning the truth she
remained on friendly terms with Athénaïs. At the same time, she was
desperately unhappy, longing only to retire to a convent of the
strictest Order where she might spend the rest of her life expiating her
mortal sin of loving the king and becoming the mother of his children.

For the next six years, the king insisted on her presence. He needed
her to conceal the grave scandal of his double adultery, and demanded
that she retain the rank of *maîtresse en titre* long after his love for her
had cooled. She and Athénaïs were obliged to live in close proximity,
travelling together, dining together, sharing the same lodgings. At
first Athénaïs did not object; perhaps she hoped to conceal the facts
from her husband, perhaps she cruelly enjoyed, as Mme de Caylus
suggests, inflicting upon her rival the kind of humiliations to which
Louise had thoughtlessly subjected the queen. However that may
have been, the two ladies were always together, and, on journeys, sat
with the queen in Her Majesty's coach, with the result that the crowds
who saw it pass boasted of having seen three queens together on the
same day.

No one was deceived. In the playhouses allusions were made that pointed very clearly to Mme de Montespan as the reigning beauty; street songs took up the theme, the gossip and rumours were endless. That arch gossip Mme de Sévigné wrote to her daughter, 'The Dew and Torrent are bound close together by the need for concealment, and every day they keep company with Fire and Ice [the king and queen]. This cannot continue long without an explosion.' But for once Mme de Sévigné was wrong; it lasted six years.

Louise bore the humiliation patiently for a long time, because the king was blissfully happy, and she loved him. But when, at one of their lodgings, she was allotted a room which provided the only access to Mme de Montespan's bedroom, and was obliged to see them pass in and out laughing and talking, with no more than a casual word thrown in her direction, it was too much. One evening, he tossed the little dog he was carrying into her lap as he went by, and then she did summon up the courage to make a gentle protest. The king replied that he had indeed fallen in love with Athénaïs, but swore that he still deeply loved Louise herself, and perhaps to prove his steadfast passion put her once again with child, which only served to increase her distress. She immediately fled to a convent; but the king, when he heard that she had gone, rode after her and brought her back himself. She made several other attempts to escape; but it was not until 1674 that he finally allowed her to retire.

As for Athénaïs, her pride would not allow her for long to take the second place. She was exceptionally courageous and quite unafraid of the king (she was indeed one of the very few not to be reduced to near-panic by his awesome majesty), and there were frequent angry scenes. Mme de Caylus describes 'one of many, in which she furiously upbraided him for indecently advertising his promiscuity. The king was very much upset and asked her pardon. "It was all unintentional," he said, "the arrangements have come about imperceptibly." "Imperceptible to you, may be," she retorted, "but very clearly visible to me."' Despite their rows, or perhaps because of them, the king adored her. Unlike Louise, she gave her whole mind to pleasing him, encouraging him in the pursuit of glory, and, most important, she took an active interest in his plans for Versailles. Glory was no empty word to Mme de Montespan; she desired it for the king her sovereign, but fully intended to share it with him and, in the meanwhile, took everything that added to her own grandeur and the huge private fortune that she was accumulating.

33. Madame de Montespan at Clagny

MME DE MONTESPAN
REACHES THE SUMMIT

The Peace of Aix-La-Chapelle, ending the war against Spain and giving Flanders to the French, was signed in 1668. The Court once more took up residence at Saint-Germain, and the king was able to turn his whole attention to Versailles. He gave his sanction to Le Vau's plan of leaving the old house untouched, but surrounding it with an envelope of new buildings. On the garden side, two high wings built of stone would contain the private apartments of the king and queen, while on the other side, where 'the little house of cards' had faced the village, there were to be new constructions in the spirit of the original, built of rose-red brick and with high, blue slate roofs.

Before the workmen took over the château and made it uninhabitable, the king gave one last festival to celebrate the peace and bid farewell to the old life. The pleasures outrivalled in beauty those of the *Plaisirs de l'Ile Enchantée*; Molière gave the first performance of his famous play *Georges Dandin*; the fireworks were more spectacular than ever before; but the tone of the festival was different. Gone were romantic themes of gallant knights saving damsels in distress, and gentle, pastoral ballets; their place was taken by a pageant, *The Triumph of Bacchus*, and the ballets celebrated the return of wealth and plenty.

The king's precious orange trees, removed from their white wooden tubs, stood everywhere in massive silver boxes; there were rich prizes for winners of the games, and cornucopias poured forth precious stones as gifts for the ladies. The king, at supper, with poor Louise, dull, tearful, pregnant with her fourth child, beside him, looked longingly down the table where bursts of laughter and excitement centred around the two most amusing ladies at the Court—the Marquise de Montespan and her crony the widow Scarron, the lady who had been overcome by the king's beauty when, eight years earlier, she had seen him bringing his bride to Paris. She later became Mme de Maintenon, and observers who lived to the end of the king's long reign used to say that at that fête, had they realized it, they saw the past, present, and future sitting together at the same table.

When the party was over, the king and Mme de Montespan settled down to enjoy their attachment to the full. This, it is said, was the moment when their union was consummated and she became his mistress in deed as well as in name. During the past year she had refused him month after month; rightly judging that to keep him in suspense increased his passion and made her power over him complete. The fact that the king went in and out of her bedroom at their lodgings during the campaign meant nothing, for at that period it was customary for ladies to receive visitors in bed, and the space between the bed and the wall—the *ruelle*—was claimed to be the place for the best and wittiest talk imaginable.

Whatever the relationship between the king and Athénaïs may have been at that time, an event occurred at the end of July which Louis XIV found intolerably embarrassing. This was the sudden arrival in Paris of the Marquis de Montespan, who appears to have believed that the moment was ripe for him to claim compensation for the loss of his wife. Mme de Caylus describes him as a wild young man with ridiculous ambitions: 'He was generally regarded as a rogue and a fool, for had he desired only his wife's return, the king, no matter how much infatuated, could not have contested his marital rights. But M. de Montespan was less concerned with those rights than with the profit he might make from their loss; and his subsequent conduct was occasioned by resentment at his failure.'

He behaved in a reckless fashion that seems to have aroused more laughter than sympathy among the courtiers. For example, he insisted on reading aloud to La Grande Mademoiselle the draft of a long speech which he swore to having inflicted on the king, quoting the Bible story of David and Bathsheba and warning of God's anger if his wife were not immediately returned. 'You must be crazy,' said Mademoiselle. 'No one will believe you capable of writing this speech. People will say that your uncle the Archbishop of Sens did it for you, for everyone knows that he is ill-disposed to Mme de Montespan.' When that lady heard the story, she merely said, 'It embarrasses me to

think that my husband, as well as my poll-parrot, is a laughing-stock for the rabble.'

M. de Montespan made angry scenes, bursting in upon his wife and reducing her to tears with torrents of abuse. The king, at first, took no action; but when he learned that Montespan had a plan to kidnap Athénaïs and take her to Spain, he had him arrested, imprisoned for a few weeks, and then banished to his country house in Gascony. Once arrived there, Montespan gave orders for both sides of the massive front door to be flung open whenever he entered or went out, saying that his cuckold's horns required the extra space. When Athénaïs gave birth to a son, he invited his friends to a wake, draping his house and his coach with black, and wearing deepest mourning, 'For my poor wife, who dies a victim to ambition and coquetry.' The last that was heard of M. de Montespan was of his leading his regiment to storm a convent in order to kidnap a nun for whom he had taken a fancy.

Once her husband was out of the way Athénaïs's only concern was to keep the king's love. She could not doubt his passion, but did not trust his fidelity, and therefore turned her whole mind to becoming indispensable. She suggested a new architect for Versailles, Jean Hardouin Mansart, nephew of the famous François Mansart who gave his name to the high slate roofs so much favoured in an earlier period. The king brought Mansart in to continue the work of Le Vau, and it was he who designed the beautiful garden-frontage of Versailles. On the façade which Le Vau had built, the wings on either side were joined by a long terrace that covered the ground floor. It was Mansart's idea, to which the king gladly consented, to fill the space above the terrace with a magnificent gallery, the *Galerie des Glaces*, the lovely Hall of Mirrors that is the pride and glory of Versailles.

It is said that the king was at Fontainebleau when Mansart showed him the first draft of his plan, and that he was so delighted that without hesitation he ordered the work to be put in hand immediately and to proceed at breakneck speed. The speed was indeed tremendous, for it seems almost incredible that no more than eight years were needed to transform the cramped little hunting-lodge of the king's father into the most magnificent palace in all Europe.

Complaints and criticism poured in both from Colbert and the courtiers. The minister deplored the terrible expense; the courtiers, for whom Versailles had no charm, grumbled at the damp, at the scenery, at the lack of accommodation in the village, at there being, in the château, no dining-room or drawing-rooms for the household, at the long, uncomfortable journey to and from Saint-Germain. What they did not foresee was that by the time the château had been made habitable, the king would have turned the hamlet of Versailles with its

34. opposite *Versailles, showing the two new wings designed by Mansart*

35. Jules Hardouin Mansart

*36. Louis XIV before the château of
Versailles*

two squalid inns into a well-planned town capable of housing ten
thousand inhabitants. The damp was not affecting his excellent health,
the gardens were magically beautiful, and he was generous in giving
grants to those wishing to build houses in the neighbourhood. At that
time he was very happy; he looked at all that he had done, and all that
he planned to do, and saw that it was good; he took up his pen and
wrote a guide book for visitors to the garden, telling them which way
to turn and where to stand in order to obtain the perfect view of every
fontain and vista.

Athénaïs, meanwhile, did not let the grass grow under her feet. She

was determined to be treasured and made the king aware, when he
tried to load her with presents, that only the very best was good
enough for her. He gave her land, at Clagny, not far from Versailles, to
build a house, and directed Mansart to draw plans; but when she saw
the result she refused it with scorn, saying it was a contemptible little
offering, the kind of thing men gave to chorus-girls; whereupon
Mansart was told to produce something on a much grander scale, and
to proceed with the work at the same breakneck speed as at Versailles.
Clagny took ten years to finish and cost nearly a million livres. It was a
source of intense pleasure both to the king and to Athénaïs, as they

discussed every detail, and watched the house and garden grow in beauty, in the hands of Mansart and the old team of Le Nôtre and Le Brun, with their hundreds of gardeners, painters, and decorators.

Mme de Sévigné saw Clagny before it was finished and was enchanted: 'Armida's palace is proceeding at a great pace,' she wrote to her daughter. 'The garden is finished already. Le Nôtre (you know his way) has arranged as a background a line of dark trees that look superb. In front is a regular forest of orange trees in exceedingly large tubs, and to hide these is a low hedge of tuberoses, roses, jasmine and pinks, a lovely, unexpected touch—everyone who sees the place is ravished by it.' One may imagine the beauty of the Clagny gardens, which, alas, no longer exist. Le Nôtre designed them with no other thought than to please, and no concern for money or labour. Athénaïs herself fell in love with them, and in one season planted eight thousand daffodils, and employed (paid by the king) twelve hundred gardeners.

Attached to Clagny was a home farm of the most elegant description. Mme de Sévigné raved over it; 'the most amorous turtle doves; the fattest pigs; cows that yield a superabundance of milk; the curliest possible lambs, and the gooseyest geese imaginable.' She was fascinated by the speed of the new favourite's rise, and reported every happening for the delectation of her daughter.

When the Court was at Saint-Germain, Athénaïs and her bosom friend, Françoise Scarron, frequently dined with Mme de Sévigné in Paris, intimate parties with no other guests, and the servants sent out of the room to allow freedom for gossip. At such times Mme Scarron appeared a different person; dropping the icy reserve that, in public, kept her lips primly sealed, she joyfully entered into the fun, with tales so comic, so nearly libellous that the ever-careful Mme de Sévigné thought it prudent to use a code when she sent letters through the post. Thus Mme de Montespan, notorious for her love of money, became *Quanto* (How much?) or *Quantova* (What price now?), from an Italian card-game that was all the rage. Françoise Scarron was *Le Dégel* (the Thaw) and the king, whose name often appeared, *The Friend*, or *The Lord of All*.

It was not only at Clagny that Mme de Montespan lived the life of which she had dreamed. Everywhere she went she was attended by the pomp and luxury that properly belonged to the Queen of France, had that unhappy lady chosen to claim it. Mme de Sévigné describes one of her journeys to join the king. '*Quanto* left for Moulins on Thursday, in a boat freshly painted and gilded, and draped in crimson damask, which the bailiff had prepared against her coming, together with thousands of banners bearing the devices of France and of Navarre. Nothing was ever prettier or more delightful, and the cost amounted to over a thousand golden crowns; but since the lady informed him that she had written to the king praising his hospitality, he will no doubt be quickly rewarded.'

Mme de Montespan, at this period, was the king's pride and joy, for her beauty was radiant and she appeared the exact image of the magnificence and charm which he desired to make the hall-mark of his Court. To him she seemed perfect and he poured money upon her, even paying, without much protest, her colossal gambling debts. She was not miserly with his money, but spent it lavishly, which he not only condoned but encouraged. 'Wherever she goes,' wrote Mme de Sévigné, 'she is expected to scatter her largesse far and wide, which she does with exemplary grace, for she is extremely open-handed.' She did not, however, seek to copy the king's graciousness, for although she opened hospitals and did her quota of good works, it was noteworthy when she was polite to visitors, and she often refused to receive ladies.

At Court, her hauteur was terrifying. She gloried in her place as the king's mistress and descended upon bores and flatterers with annihilating remarks that were never afterwards forgotten, because of their wit. The king enjoyed the joke as much as any, for she was wise enough to spare the people whom he liked. She had set herself to study him during the months when she held him at bay; and thus, when her moment came, she knew him through and through, and how best to please and support him. One of the qualities he most prized in her was her readiness to do what he wished, at all times. She was never fatigued or ailing, and in all her nine pregnancies she never pleaded indisposition to avoid travelling, or let it dim her brightness. There was never a moment when she wearied him.

37. The château and garden of Clagny

Another thing that especially endeared Athénaïs to Louis XIV and raised her high in his esteem was her absolute refusal to accept from him presents of jewellery. He thought her wonderfully modest and high-minded and, in 1674, writing to Colbert from his army's headquarters, he said, 'Mme de Montespan resolutely refuses to let me give her jewellery. So that she may not feel the want of it, I wish you to have made a pretty jewel-case, of a size to hold the following *parures*'—(and he gave a list of sets in every variety of precious stone). 'You will think her attitude very odd; but she will not listen to reason in this matter of presents.'

It is sometimes said that Athénaïs was being purely mercenary in this matter, well knowing that the jewels the king gave would be of far less value than those he lent; but she understood his strangely possessive love of precious stones, and the wrench it was to him when he felt obliged to give them away. He had never forgotten his humiliation at the time of his marriage, when his pride had been shattered by the contrast between the magnificent *parures* brought from Spain by Marie Thérèse, and the noticeably less costly sets of jewellery which were all the French treasury could afford. Since that time he had built up a collection of jewels which he treasured for their value and beauty, and of which he dispossessed himself with the greatest reluctance.

Such forbearance in his mistress struck him as a proof of her love and understanding, and made him still more generous in gifts of money which she took without hesitation. Feeling secure in his love, she next set about providing herself with an establishment and a wealthy family. She bought a house in Paris, paid her debts, and persuaded the king to give advancement to all her near relations. Her father, the Duc de Mortemart, became Governor of Paris, drawing a vast income from dues on merchandise brought in or out of the city. Her brother, the Duc de Vivonne, rose to being captain-general of the galleys; her sister was made Abbess of Fontevrault, one of the richest convents in France, and for her penniless niece, the abbess's daughter, the king found a wealthy husband in Mazarin's nephew, the Duc de Nevers. To this young man, of questionable morals, Louis XIV gave so many highly paid jobs that he amassed the equivalent of a princely dowry.

Her base secured, Athénaïs proceeded to please the king in every possible way and further all his wishes. She gloried in her place at the top, providing, according to Mme de Sévigné, 'the very image of triumphant beauty', a tribute to the king's taste in women, and a welcome contrast to the timidity of Louise. She delighted him by making of herself a walking advertisement of the excellence of French

fashions, for she dressed magnificently and the effect was overwhelming. One of her dresses has become famous. It was of cloth of gold, embroidered with gold thread, bordered with gold and overlaid with gold brocade mingled with still more cloth of gold. 'A dress', wrote Primi Visconti, 'that the fairies must have fashioned for no human hand could have embroidered it.'

Yet there was a flaw that marred her otherwise perfectly beautiful appearance, one which the king, in other days, would have minded very much, for she was neither very clean nor neat. It was the sweet-natured Louise who came to her rescue, tying her ribbons with dextrous fingers, curling her hair into ringlets and setting it in a style so becoming that the queen adopted it, declaring that she was certainly not copying Mme de Montespan, but doing it to please the king who thought that curls were very pretty.

To Louise de La Vallière, Athénaïs was sweetness itself, always kind and loving, never an angry word, encircling her with a protective arm as they walked in the gardens of Versailles or Saint-Germain. The courtiers could not understand why Louise still appeared miserable. The king had made her a rich duchess and had not dismissed her, she was still handsome and in the prime of life, moreover she appeared to have the friendship of the new favourite. Why did she not rouse herself to enjoy her advantages and begin a new life? But the friendship of Mme de Montespan was no joy to Louise. What she pined for was the love of the king, and she suffered cruelly when he ignored her and went eagerly to join her rival. For three more years she endured the humiliation of being used as a screen to hide from the public her loved one's mortal sin of double adultery, and then, in 1674, he let her go where she longed to be, to the Convent of the Carmelites, there to expiate the sins of her past life by penance and mortification of the flesh. 'What I shall suffer with the Carmelites', she said, 'will serve to remind me of the cruel pain that those people inflicted on me.'

She took the veil under the name Sister Louise de la Miséricorde. Mme de Sévigné reported that she was 'as beautiful and as courageous as ever, and bore herself with remarkable dignity and charm.' There were many onlookers who were moved by her dignity; 'I think I never saw her looking more lovely or more at peace,' wrote Mlle de Scudéry. 'She should be happy, if only for not having to lace up Mme de Montespan's corsets. If the truth were told, she would be recognized as a genuine martyr.'

When Louise had departed, Athénaïs turned for advice and sympathy to her old friend the widow Scarron, six years older than herself. That lady had been left in straitened circumstances after her husband's death, and was living in rented rooms at one of the Paris convents, without a house of her own, without a carriage, and without servants, save for Nanon Balbien, an old peasant-woman who had been her mother's maid. Yet Mme Scarron had good friends among the most highly respected of the nobility, and dined in the best houses. In her husband's time she had entertained the cream of Parisian literary society, and was herself one of its most admired members, noted for her witty conversation, her good looks and elegant appearance. Her intimate friends included Mme de Sévigné, Mlle de Scudéry, a writer much praised by *Les Précieuses*, and Ninon de l'Enclos, the famous courtesan. What is more she did not lack for beaux since it became the fashion for the young bucks in that circle to think themselves in love with her. No one dared to patronize her, for her pride and wit kept the impudent at bay, while her perfect manners made her acceptable to the well-bred.

Mme Scarron, despite her poverty, had a genius for dress. She wore plain dresses of the best grey silk that she could afford, so elegantly and perfectly fitting that they appeared beyond the reach of fashion and enhanced the prettiness of her figure and her beautiful black eyes. The effect was so startling that her strict confessor rebuked her for dressing too smartly. 'But M. l'Abbé,' replied Mme Scarron, 'I do not wear rich silks.' 'That is true,' said he, 'but when you kneel, so much silk falls around me that I feel it to be too worldly.'

Worldly she may have been; but her dominating passion was a rigid

39. *Madame de
Maintenon and her
niece*

devotion to respectability, as she describes in a 'self-portrait', written a
few years later at the command of her confessor. 'I have a morality',
she wrote, 'and a tendency towards virtue that prevents me from
doing wrong. I love to be respected and well-liked, which puts me on
my guard against my passions. Thus I rarely need to reproach myself
for sins committed, but rather for very human weaknesses—much
vanity, a strong inclination to frivolity and pleasure, a propensity to
judge others, and a reticence occasioned only by prudence.'

She was a deeply religious woman. She would not have lied to her
confessor, and her pursuit of respectability was no pretence. It was

engendered by firm morality and, what is more, provided a much needed defence for an attractive young widow living unprotected in a world regarded in those days as being excessively immoral. It may not have been hard for her to live a virtuous life for she is said to have been frigid and incapable of passion. 'I did not want to be loved by any one person,' she said in later years; 'my whole desire was to be liked and respected by the best people. That was my ideal, and I therefore held myself on a very tight rein, which cost me nothing, provided I kept my good name. That was all I cared about.' Fénelon said of her that she was cold and dry; Ninon de l'Enclos that she had no aptitude for the arts of love. 'She was virtuous because she had no courage. I tried to change her, but she was too much concerned with morality.'

The scandalous stories of her debauchery at the time of her marriage to Scarron were not current then. They seem to have been put about by her enemies after she had become Mme de Maintenon, the most feared and envied woman in France. They were based on the flimsiest evidence and her intimacy with the noble ladies of the pious set would seem to contradict them. Only one such story, her supposed love affair with the Marquis de Villarceaux, her husband's friend, is at all credible, for he certainly possessed the portrait of a beautiful young woman stepping naked from her bath, and her face bore a striking likeness to Françoise Scarron. But whether the portrait was really her likeness, or whether she posed for it, remains a mystery. Considering her passion for respectability and the care she took of her good name, it all seems most unlikely; she would not have done anything so foolish.

That she and Mme de Montespan should have been cronies for so many years may seem strange, but it is not incomprehensible. To begin with, they thoroughly enjoyed being together. Witty, well-bred, lively, frivolous, experts in the art of delivering sallies and repartee, they struck sparks from one another, and on the tedious journeys, following the king to the wars, their coach rang with laughter. But merriment was not their only bond: Athénaïs was nervous and insecure, not afraid of the king who obviously adored her, but afraid of one day losing his love, and of a future enclosed in a convent or sent back to a husband who hated her. Mme Scarron could be kind to her friends, and her practical commonsense was a comfort and support. She dearly loved to give advice, accompanied by little pious homilies to which she gave an amusing twist that made them irresistibly funny. She seems increasingly to have believed that she had a god-given mission to save the souls of those whom she thought worth saving, and Athénaïs, guilty of adultery in such exalted company, was manifestly a candidate for her best efforts.

She treated that lady with supreme tact and a touch of respect that was much appreciated. Tact and respect were, indeed, essential, for Athénaïs, as proud as Lucifer, was always on the look-out for slights, and liable to outbursts of temper, of which the king was a frequent victim. The courtiers had become accustomed to shrieks and cries of anger coming from her room; objects were thrown with force, and those who used the path beneath her windows referred to their passage as 'coming under the bombardment'. It may be that Athénaïs frightened herself on these occasions, for the scenes were usually succeeded by weeping and black sulks. At first, the king enjoyed his power to bring her round and make the sun shine again; but latterly, as had happened with Louise, he had shown signs of boredom, and, although he did her the signal honour of legitimating their three children, she could not be certain that his eye was not already straying. In these difficult times she depended more and more on Françoise Scarron's advice, and being, as Saint-Simon says, a good friend to the very few whom she took in friendship, she looked about for some way of doing her a good turn.

The opportunity came in 1673 when the king publicly acknowledged their children. He loved the idea of family life; but there were difficulties, for the Church viewed with horror his attachment to Mme de Montespan, a married woman. The affair had been known to exist for the past five years, there were as yet no signs of the rupture which religion demanded, and he was accordingly refused the sacraments. Louis XIV, however, was not much disturbed by the prelates. He had returned triumphant from the war; moreover, his health being excellent, he had few qualms at being refused absolution;

40. A ballet by Lulli performed before the royal family at Versailles

as for missing Communion at Easter, there would, he felt sure, be ample time for him to repent at leisure.

Another problem was less easily disposed of. The fact of their having three children had hitherto been kept a profound secret. Athénaïs had appeared in public until the last possible moment, and in the case of the latest baby had been seen, in Court dress, beside the king just two days after its birth. After being acknowledged as his offspring, their existence could no longer be denied, and the effect on M. de Montespan was unpredictable, for that madman might take it into his head to have his revenge by claiming his wife's children as his own, thus creating a still more horrifying scandal.

That particular danger was, however, averted, for M. de Montespan made no move. The Grand Mademoiselle reported in her *Mémoires*: 'The king has declared himself to be the father of three children born out of wedlock; two boys, one of whom will be entitled the Duc du Maine, the other the Comte de Vexin, and a girl who will be known as Mlle de Nantes. In the deed of legitimation the mother's name is not given.'

The question of the children's upbringing next had to be considered, and this was where Athénaïs thought that her friend might be rewarded. The children needed to be raised in a manner befitting their royal birth, and a lady of the highest quality, and above all discreet, must be found to act as their governess. Françoise Scarron had all the right experience, for she had, at times, supervised the noble households of Mme d'Albret, the Duchesse de Richelieu, and Mme de Montchevreuil whom she called 'my good friend' and at whose country house she stayed each summer. 'I took care of her household,' wrote Françoise many years later, 'looked after her accounts and all her housekeeping expenses . . . I always had her children around me. I taught one of them to read, another the catechism, indeed, I taught them all I knew myself.'

Thus the widow Scarron appeared to Athénaïs a perfect choice, for not only was she very good with children, but she badly needed the generous salary, the house, servants and comforts that the position would bring. Athénaïs mentioned her name to the king, only to find that he strongly objected. He could not abide the woman, he said. She was a prude and a blue-stocking; he felt her disapproval every time she approached him, and her pious and strait-laced friends were the kind of people he most disliked. In the end, however, he accepted the idea for the sake of peace, and Athénaïs dispatched Mme d'Heudicourt, a mutual friend, to impart the glorious news. She met with a flat refusal. Mme Scarron was disinclined to accept the care of Mme de Montespan's bastards. It was none the less a hard decision, for she

41. Louis XIV attending a lesson given to the Dauphin

needed the money, and secretly longed for a post at Court, no matter how humble.

A consultation with her confessor provided the solution. If she received the king's command to take charge of his children she would be bound to obey. She might then ignore Mme de Montespan's part in the affair, accept the post, and still retain the respect of the pious set. That command Louis XIV was most unwilling to give, but at last he consented. A comfortable house was bought and sufficient money provided; but he acted under protest, on condition of never having to see or hear further mention 'of a hussy for whom too much has already been done'.

One of the greatest attractions of the post for Françoise Scarron was the thought of caring for children, for this strange and childless woman, to whom the sexual act was intensely displeasing, gave to other people's children all the love of which she was capable. All her life she had some child or other living happily with her, and when she was over eighty she wrote to the hesitant mother of a little girl whom she had invited to stay, 'Do send her, children never tire me.'

It was in a nursery that she was at her most charming, full of fun and loving kindness, with children around her and on her knee, listening

77

42. Madame de Montespan with her children

to the kind of stories they most enjoyed, many of which began, 'When I was a little girl,' and contained a comforting and practical moral. She cuddled them, and very soothingly brushed their hair, making gentle fun of them with a maternal affection that won their hearts. The icy reserve with which she protected herself in Society thawed in the presence of children, and the air was full of laughter.

There was much to do to the house before it was fit for occupation, and meanwhile the three children lived in the homes of their wet-nurses. Françoise visited them daily, and personally supervised the task of redecoration and improvement. Many years later she delighted the girls at Saint-Cyr, the famous school that she founded, by telling them of her troubles at that time. 'The somewhat dubious honour brought hard work and great responsibilities. I was often obliged to climb ladders in order to hang the curtains, for secrecy had to be maintained and workmen were not allowed in the house. I had no help from the wet-nurses; they would not lift a finger, saying their milk would be spoiled if they fatigued themselves. I used often to go on foot and poorly dressed from one of their houses to another, carrying parcels of meat or clean linen, and when the children were poorly, I sat up with them all through the night. Early next day I would return to the house, entering by the back door. Then, after dressing for Society, I would step out of the front door and into my carriage and visit Mme d'Albret or the Duchesse de Richelieu, in order to prevent my friends from imagining that I had something to conceal.'

In spite of all precautions, Françoise's friends could not help seeing that life had become easier for her. Mme de Sévigné wrote that she came to supper nearly every evening. 'We thought it would be amusing to drive her back to her house at midnight, at the far end of the Faubourg Saint-Germain, much beyond where Mme de La Fayette lives. It is a fine large house which no one is allowed to enter, and has beautiful rooms and a big garden. She now has a carriage and horses, and many servants; moreover, though she still dresses quietly, she is supremely elegant, like someone who spends her life with the best people. She is still charming, beautiful, kind, and anxious to be of service.'

Françoise was at this time very happy, for she had work which she enjoyed and did supremely well and money was no longer a problem. Her ideas about the upbringing of young children were far in advance of her time; she believed in firm rules, fresh air, early bedtime, and plain wholesome food. She gave the king's children the kind of affection which their real mother was very far from bestowing on them. Athénaïs's tendency was to ignore them. She liked children to be decorative, well-mannered, and amusing—flattering reflections of her beautiful self, but in no way competing for attention or diverting the king's notice. At first the appointment of Françoise had been a complete success; she was so quietly competent, so discreet as to be virtually unnoticeable; but even she was not perfection, for there were times when she plagued Athénaïs for instructions. There was, for example, the incident of the nursery-chimney catching fire. Françoise had sent an urgent message to Saint-Germain—should she send for the fire-brigade or not? Left alone, the entire house might go up in flames; if firemen came, they would certainly guess the children's identity. What should she do? The messenger returned with the great lady's reply, 'Delighted to hear of the fire. It will bring the children luck.'

When they were with her and being good, Athénaïs pressed sweets upon them, kept them up long past their bedtimes, covered them with kisses. If they were sick or cried, she blamed their governess and complained to the king, who refused to interfere. He was genuinely fond of his children, and gave them his love in a way that he found impossible with his other son the dauphin, who belonged not to him but to the nation and was brought up in a separate establishment. What was more, his opinion of Françoise Scarron was changing for the better. He had been moved by her grief at the death of his little daughter. He also had felt the loss, and he took to paying unexpected visits to the two boys in the nursery which he found cosy and peaceful, a haven of refuge after one of Mme de Montespan's furies.

On one such visit the king's eye was greeted with the most charming scene imaginable. He saw Mme Scarron, still young, attractive, prettily dressed and deliciously scented. She was sitting smiling among a group of children, with the baby Duc de Vexin in her lap, her arm around the Duc du Maine, and a little girl, Mme d'Heudicourt's daughter, holding her other hand. They all four looked as happy and as cosy as it was possible to be, and the king turned to the gentleman who accompanied him, saying, 'She knows how to love, it would be delightful to be loved by her.'

After a time, Athénaïs began to view the king's visits to the nursery with increasing disfavour. Not that she was jealous—no possible cause, it seemed, for that—but they were said to include serious conversations in which religion and morals were frequently discussed, and of that she did not approve. There seemed only one thing to do, to persuade Françoise to resign. Dismissal was out of the question in view of the great service she had rendered, and Athénaïs accordingly set out to make life a misery for her old friend, taunting her with her inferior position, threatening constant complaints to the king. There were tears and many angry scenes, and Françoise was indeed made wretched.

Poor Françoise, on the one hand she genuinely longed for retirement and quiet religious peace, on the other, she had fallen in love with the little Duc du Maine and he badly needed her care. He had been a sickly baby, and when he was three years old had developed a stiff leg that had not grown to match the other. It was said that his wet-nurse had dropped him; but he may well have had spinal paralysis. However that may have been, the doctors' treatment was sheer torture, for they stretched him on a miniature rack in a vain effort to lengthen the shorter leg. The little boy was patient, brave, and very pathetic, clinging ever more closely to the kind governess who loved and encouraged him.

Thus torn, she wrote to her confessor for advice. 'M. le Duc du Maine does not improve, and this continues to distress me although his life is not in danger. It is always afflicting to see those whom one loves in pain; but what disturbs me is the realization that I love this child as much as I did the little girl who died. The folly of it so angers me that I weep during the whole of mass. Nothing could be more foolish than such immoderate love for a child who is not my own, whom I may never claim as mine, whose affection in the course of time will cause me mortal pain and displease those to whom he legally belongs. How absurd of me to continue in this unhappy condition. Only a slave would refuse to make the change that would bring peace of mind.'

At this point Mme de Montespan changed her tactics and tried to buy Françoise off with marriage to a duke, albeit 'a somewhat unsavoury and poverty-stricken nobleman', who pronounced himself willing to be married in exchange for a handsome dowry. When that offer was indignantly refused, Athénaïs suggested a rich abbey. The king, she said, would make no difficulty of endowing her with the next one to fall vacant. It was a life Françoise would enjoy, and well within her capabilities. But the king, when this idea was put to him, thought differently. He would not let Mme Scarron retire from the Court; but at the same time understood Athénaïs's desire to see less of her. His solution to the problem was to buy for Françoise a pretty château, on a small estate named Maintenon, not far from Chartres, and he sent Le Nôtre to improve the garden for her. The estate was a marquisate; its owner bore that title, and thus by its ownership the poor widow Scarron became Marquise de Maintenon, taking the first step on the steep ascent that led, ten years later, to the unimaginable height of becoming the king's wife.

In the end it was the four-year-old Duc du Maine who clinched matters for Françoise. The king, who had become fond of him, expressed a wish to see him quite alone, without the protection of servants or his governess. This was something he could never have attempted with the thirteen-year-old dauphin, a victim of the brutal training meted out, by tradition, to heirs apparent so as to deter them from rebellion. That poor child shook with terror in his father's presence and remained totally bereft of speech. With the Duc du Maine it was different. He faced the ordeal of a conversation with the king in high spirits, answering so brightly and reasonably that his father was astonished. 'How comes it that you are so sensible?' he asked. 'It must be my governess,' replied the little boy. 'She is the very image of good sense.'

That settled the matter. Françoise continued in her post, and she

and the children moved to Saint-Germain, where the king and their mother saw them every day, which gave the occasion for more angry scenes. In the spring of 1676, the recently ennobled Marquise de Maintenon, now of sufficient rank to act as the escort of royal children, gained the king's permission to take the Duc du Maine on a tour of the famous watering-places in the south-west of France, more especially to Barèges, where it was hoped to find a cure for all his disabilities— his boils and dermatitis, and his ungainly limp. They travelled in royal style and were away for six months, during which time Françoise hugely enjoyed herself, and the little duke's lameness and general health were much improved.

When they returned to Saint-Germain they found that peace had been restored. Mme de Sévigné wrote to her daughter, '*L'Ami* and *l'Amie*' (her code names for the king and Athénaïs) 'spent the entire day together, and when *La Femme* returned to Paris they dined together . . . In short, all is serene and jealousy a thing of the past.'

THE PURSUIT OF GLORY

eyond all doubt, my ruling passion is the pursuit of glory,' wrote Louis XIV in 1668, when he was thirty years old, and his yearning for glory was constantly fed by fulsome flattery. Very early in his reign, his ministers, generals and courtiers discovered that pretended agreement was the quickest way to gain his consent; and they went further, persuading him that their best ideas came from him, and that he had an instinct for statecraft and military strategy that far exceeded the value of their professional experience.

During a succession of unnecessary wars in the early part of his reign, his brilliant generals had brought him extraordinary success, for which he took personal credit. From 1667 until 1678 there had been a series of victorious campaigns in the Netherlands, culminating in the Peace of Nijmegen by the terms of which the power and glory of France were greatly increased. Every spring he had joined his army at the beginning of the season, tearing himself away from Le Nôtre and his beloved garden; but not from the ladies by whom he loved to be surrounded. He needed women about him to provide an audience and share with him the honours of victory, so every year, with the queen at their head, they followed him in a long procession of coaches to the frontier, where, despite Colbert's protests at the vast expense incurred, they were lodged with their servants in one or other of the neighbouring towns.

Woe betide the lady who complained of fatigue or discomfort! She was the king's honoured guest, fed and lodged at his expense, and it was her bounden duty to show pride and pleasure. Malingerers were sent home in disgrace, for grumbles and sulky faces spoiled the king's enjoyment and were therefore unforgivable, no matter what the cause. Thus everyone appeared cheerful, and when the king joined the ladies in the evening there was laughter, card playing, and good conversation, in which he himself took part, telling amusing tales of army life.

Louis XIV thoroughly enjoyed life with the army, living under canvas among his officers, sharing their rations and occasionally their dangers, and presiding over councils of war. There was plenty of

44. The siege of
Maastricht

work for him to do of the kind that he loved, for the generals kept him busy revising the drill and discipline, studying changes in regimental uniforms, making swift decisions on a mass of tiny details. He read and initialled all dispatches to the war office, and scribbled notes in the margin for Colbert's attention; but what he most enjoyed was reviewing his troops before the ladies of the Court party, and he did it so often that he came to be known abroad as 'the reviewing king'. He was indeed a splendid sight, for he had the advantage of a handsome face and a good figure and was a superb horseman. This he knew well, and he loved to receive the soldiers' cheers as he rode down the lines in his famous hat with the scarlet feathers. He was popular with the troops, who were well paid and well cared for, and he could not have enough of their acclaim.

But of all military ceremonies, the one from which the king gained the greatest satisfaction was taking the surrender at the end of a siege, when the defeated garrison marched out with all the honours of war 'bag and baggage, drums beating, flags flying, matches lit, bullet in the cheek.' When that supreme moment arrived, the king took the salute and afterwards held a grand review, watched by the ladies who had followed him.

At such times Athénaïs came into her element. Radiantly lovely, exquisitely dressed, attracting all the attention that should rightly have been centred on the queen, she talked and smiled, the image of graciousness, and the king's heart was filled with the glory of having the cleverest and most beautiful woman in the world for his mistress.

But he was growing restless and, as time went on, his fancy strayed to other women. Perhaps, though he welcomed the results, he found her frequent pregnancies a nuisance, for inevitably they interfered with his pleasure; moreover during them she lost much of her beauty and became unattractively stout. Perhaps his terrible zest for the sexual act became insatiable. However that may have been, he was for a time shamefully promiscuous. Not only did he sleep every night with the queen, and every evening with Athénaïs, but he carelessly involved himself with other women—with Athénaïs's pretty young handmaid Mlle des Oeillets; with the lovely red-headed Princesse de Soubise, said to owe her delicate pallor to a diet of veal, chicken, and fruit; to Mme du Ludres, unmarried, but addressed as Madame on account of being a canoness of Poussay Abbey. That is to list only a few; many other names were mentioned.

Athénaïs, on the whole, bore these affairs calmly. According to Mme de Caylus, she only mentioned them when joking or in a bad temper; but she was exceedingly worried about her personal appearance, for she had become so enormously stout that a bystander seeing her step into the king's coach remarked that her ankles were as big as his thighs. The king did not seem to mind. She was the only lady chosen to accompany him and the queen to the siege of Ghent, in 1678; but after a few weeks she was obliged to retire to Clagny for the birth of her last child by the king, a boy who was entitled the Comte de Toulouse. She then extended her holiday by going to Bourbon for a slimming cure. The courtiers predicted her imminent downfall, but she returned half the size glowing with beauty and good health.

'*Quantova*', said Mme de Sévigné, 'holds herself as straight as a ramrod. Quite seriously, I find her beauty radiant. She is much thinner; but this has in no way spoiled her complexion, eyes, or lips. She was wearing a dress of French point-lace, with her hair in hundreds of little curls, the two longest hanging down on either side of her face, intertwined with black ribbon. Her pearls, borrowed from Mme la Maréchale de l'Hôpital who was renowned for her magnificent jewellery, were set off by twists and festoons of priceless diamonds. Everyone was staring at her, surrounded as she was by ambassadors and the admiration of all beholders. You will scarcely believe how they rejoice at her return, or the vitality and beauty that she displays.' And Mme de Sévigné went on to say that if only

45. The king, wearing his famous red plumes, at the battle near the Bruges canal

Athénaïs were wise enough to control her temper, she would become so powerful, so famous that she would be accounted a goddess.

Athénaïs, meanwhile, was indeed in the seventh heaven. Exulting in her return to favour, she saw no need to fear rivalry, and was kindly condescending to little Mme du Ludres in the queen's drawing-room, retying her ribbons, and offering advice on a more becoming hair-style. The truth was that the king, although he succumbed to nearly every pretty face, did not find other women as lively or as amusing, and so returned with infinite satisfaction to the stimulating company of his old love. They laughed and joked together, drove out alone in the afternoon, comparing notes on their gardens and, on long journeys, travelled tête-à-tête in the king's coach while the queen followed behind with ladies of her household.

She became recognized in foreign countries as being the most important figure at the Court of Saint-Germain, and ambassadors arriving with presents for Their Majesties took to bringing, as a matter of course, equally valuable gifts for the *maîtresse en titre*. An African envoy, ignorant of the niceties of the situation, directed his master's princely gift to 'the king's assistant wife', which aroused the courtiers' mirth.

'Oh! my dear child, what a triumph!' wrote Mme de Sévigné. 'What a renewal of her arrogance! How firmly established! Joy even increased by the long history of absences and quarrels! What a return to supreme power! I spent yesterday a whole hour in her company. She was lying in bed fully dressed and painted, taking her repose before a midnight supper party. Just imagine a picture of pride and vanity and you will not be far from the truth.' Her arrogance, indeed, knew no bounds, for she lived in greater state than the queen who twice visited her at Clagny, and Primi Visconti tells how, even in Her Majesty's presence, duchesses and princesses stood up when she entered a room and did not sit down again until she had given the sign.

The courtiers seem to have tolerated, even admired her for thus displaying her power; but she went altogether too far when she descended, all jewels, silks, and smiles, upon Louise de La Vallière at the convent of the Carmelites. 'Are they making you quite comfortable?' she asked. 'Not comfortable,' replied Louise, enduring the torment of a hair shirt, 'but they make me happy.' Athénaïs closed the interview by asking her to pray for the king, and Louise withdrew, saying quietly, 'If that is your desire.' The great lady's next move was to treat the nuns to a lottery with prizes for them all, after which she sat down to dinner with them and, finding their food unappetizing, sent out a servant to buy butter, cream, wine and spices with which she made them a rich sauce. She then departed, deeply pitying them for the discomforts of religious life, and distributing with generous hands parcels of sweet cakes and chocolate.

Was this visit to her predecessor a sign of her feeling none too secure in the midst of her triumph? If so, the sudden return of Mme de Maintenon accompanied by the Duc du Maine in glowing health, who, though he still limped, was walking freely and without pain, may not have been any comfort to her. The king, who had not expected them back so soon, was moved to tears when he saw Françoise quietly standing at the back of the room and the excited child coming towards

46. The entry of Louis XIV and Marie Thérèse into Arras

him eager and unafraid. His gratitude was deep and sincere. He not only thanked her personally, but sent Louvois to convey the nation's gratitude.

When she went for a few weeks' holiday to her château at Maintenon, he actually paid her a surprise visit, an unheard-of honour that might have discomposed any ordinary woman. She, however, remained perfectly calm, welcomed him without undue fuss, and offered him a picnic in her pretty garden, with 'fish from the stream, new-laid eggs, country butter, a simple salad, fresh fruit, and most delicious little cakes'. She gave him also what he most needed: friendship, quiet talk, and peace of mind, for he was beginning to grow tired of transitory love affairs, and ashamed of his recent excesses.

To the fury of Athénaïs, he insisted on Françoise making a third in their hitherto private drives and walks. On every long journey he seated her on his other side in his coach, and one may well imagine the blood of both ladies being at boiling point, though they thought it prudent to control themselves and concentrate on pleasing and amusing the king. It was said that on the occasions when they had the royal coach to themselves, for instance on their way to join the king on the frontier, they called a truce and, as in earlier days, spent happy hours in laughter and gossip. When the carriage stopped and the steps were lowered for them to step out, their faces were set in frozen hauteur and they did not speak to one another again until the next excursion.

If Mme de Montespan was dismayed by the return of Mme de Maintenon and the relish that the king showed for her company, Françoise was shocked by that lady's arrogance, and horrified by the public display of her adultery with the king. She felt that she could no longer bring herself to take orders from the mother of his bastards or tolerate her rudeness, though she still willingly obeyed their royal father's requests. Torn between anger and loyalty, she was uncertain what to do and extremely unhappy. 'My life here is unbearable,' she wrote to her confessor. 'If I followed my own inclinations, I should

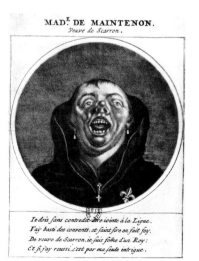

47. One of the many lampoons on Madame de Maintenon, the Widow Scarron

48. Madame de Maintenon at prayer, 1697

never cease to beg for retirement.' Six months later she was less positive. 'When I was out of favour you advised me not to leave at so bad a time. Now that I have become so much loved I cannot easily tear myself away from those who hold me to them by kindness and affection. It is far harder to loosen bonds of this nature than to force a rupture by violence.'

Throughout the winter and spring of 1678 she thus continued, at one moment determined to retire, and the next unable to bear the thought of separation. If only God would make plain His will, it would all be easy, and she wrote once more to the Abbé Gobelin asking for expert advice. What he replied is not known for certain; but he appears to have found the problem too difficult, for, in her next letter, she said 'Pray God on my behalf, since he does not permit you to do more for me.'

One decision she did manage to make. She refused to take into her care any further fruits of the double adultery, and when the last two babies appeared in 1677 and 1678 she showed her abhorrence so clearly that the king fought shy of asking her to mother them, and they were handed over to Mme de Louvois whose husband had succeeded Colbert as minister for works and buildings.

In the following winter an event occurred so alarming that

*49. The Princesse
de Soubise*

Françoise and Athénaïs were temporarily drawn together. This was
the king's sudden infatuation for a beautiful young girl of eighteen, a
newly appointed maid of honour to Madame, the king's sister-in-law,
who, being exceptionally plain, surrounded herself with a beauty
chorus in order to attract his visits.

Marie Angélique de Fontanges, this newcomer to the Court, was
tall, blonde, and graceful in all her movements. She is reputed to be the
greatest beauty ever seen at the Court of Louis XIV, and also the
silliest; 'as lovely as an angel,' said the courtiers, 'and as stupid as an
owl.' She is said to have arrived with one fixed ambition in her
otherwise empty head: to make the king her lover, oust Mme de
Montespan, and reign supreme in her stead.

Françoise, who first saw the danger, launched an agonized appeal to
the Abbé Gobelin: 'You know how much I have needed your prayers
in the past. Once again I write to entreat you to pray and have prayers
said for me; also to pray and have prayers said for the king, who teeters
on the edge of a precipice.' Alas it was too late. Beauty and
determination had conquered him, he had become inflamed with love.
Within a week of meeting Marie Angélique he had become her lover;
within a month she was the possessor of a private sitting-room at

Versailles. It was brilliantly illuminated both day and night; but next to it was a secret chamber, approached by a staircase hidden behind the panelling of the king's bedroom.

Mlle de Fontanges was not one to hide her triumph. The airs she gave herself were inconceivable, designed to outdo Mme de Montespan and to humiliate the queen, which was something that the king, despite his passion, did not relish. She drove in a dove-coloured coach drawn by eight horses (the queen's prerogative, and hers alone), and when, on her becoming pregnant, he made her a duchess, she took to copying the regal gesture with which Mme de Montespan permitted other duchesses to be seated. It may appear strange that those noble dames did not dare to protest; but the king's infatuation was such that they feared her power.

Mme de Maintenon did all she could to restrain Athénaïs; but to no avail. On 15 March, 1680, after a furious quarrel with the king, she packed her trunks and left the Court, swearing never to return. Within a month, however, she was back again, the king having appointed her Superintendent of the queen's Household, the highest post open to women. It carried a duchess's precedence and the right to a tabouret, and would certainly have included the title, had not M. de Montespan indignantly refused to accept a dukedom.

She returned still consumed with jealousy and hurt pride, for she saw that the king no longer loved her and had retrieved her only in appreciation of their once glorious partnership. Moreover his apparent affection for Françoise de Maintenon increasingly enraged her, for he had taken to spending two hours in her room every evening, chatting with her in so intimate a fashion that she was fast becoming one of the most envied ladies at the Court.

The atmosphere at Saint-Germain was thus tense and to most people disagreeable, yet there were fascinating scenes to be witnessed. Primi Visconti describes how, at mass on Sunday mornings, the congregation were regaled by the sight of Mme de Montespan and her children in the gallery on the left-hand side and the Duchesse de Fontanges in the same position on the right. It was a sight never to be forgotten when both ladies reverently told their beads, praying, like the saints, with their eyes cast heavenwards. 'Truly,' concluded Visconti, 'Court life provides the funniest scenes imaginable.'

Madame's aunt, the Duchess of Osnabrück, witnessed a similar event. She thought Mme de Montespan looked very sour and unhappy, while the newly created Duchesse de Fontanges appeared radiant, 'using her prayerbook as an excuse to look down on the king, whom she probably loves more than the King of Kings—but, indeed, the King of France is also worthy of adoration.'

The glory of the new duchess was short-lived for, as might have been predicted, the foolish girl over-stepped the mark. It happened on New Year's Day, 1681, when she attended mass wearing a dress of the same material and colour as the king's coat, and over it a wide ribbon of pale blue silk to match his Saint-Esprit. This was considered monstrous, insolent beyond all bounds, and very close to being sacrilegious. The courtiers were deeply shocked, and even the king was annoyed, to the extent of requesting Mme de Maintenon to visit the young lady and persuade her to be more discreet.

Françoise was incensed. Had the king asked her to help him terminate the affair with all kindness to the other party, she could have considered it an answer to her prayers. But termination was not what he wanted; he merely wished to use her to pacify and restrain his partner in adultery. He showed himself deaf to all her homilies and reproaches, and made her feel that she had failed in her God-sent mission to bring him to repentance. None the less, she arranged to pay the visit, arming herself with kindly advice, moral precepts, and appeals to take temptation from the king's reach and save his immortal soul.

She was emphatically the wrong person to choose for such a mission, for though she could be sweetness itself with little children, she had no pity for their elder sisters, and where love was concerned she was like a block of stone. By her own admission, she never in her life fell in love, and Fénelon, at one time her spiritual director, accused her of showing no sympathy to those who thought differently from herself, which was certainly the case with Marie Angélique de Fontanges. We have her own account of the dismal failure of her visit. 'I was with her for two hours,' she wrote, 'and I spent the whole time endeavouring to persuade her that it would be noble and praiseworthy to separate from the king. But I recollect that she exclaimed excitedly "You speak of throwing off a passion as though it were no more than changing a shift."'

No further action was taken; but the king's love for Marie Angélique had already cooled. The poor girl's pregnancy was advancing and, to his intense annoyance, it did not become her. She was tearful, complaining, always tired; and women in that condition exasperated him. He was fifty-two years old, not feeling well and once more, for the time being, sick of love. For lovely Marie Angélique the end was swift and tragic. Her baby was born dead a few weeks later, and as a result of internal bleeding she fell into an irreversible decline, a state of plaintive sickliness which he found intolerable. Since the doctors gave no hope of her recovery she was moved from Versailles to the Convent of Port Royal, which was considered a better place in which to die.

50. The Duchesse de Fontanges

The king visited her just once, when he was hunting in the
neighbourhood, and when he saw her pitiable condition he was
moved to tears. She expired a few weeks later, and is reported to have
murmured that she died happy because she had seen her king weep for
her. She was not yet twenty-one. There was a post-mortem, rather
against the king's wishes, because rumour had it that Athénaïs, in

51. Madame de Montespan

jealous rage, had caused her to be poisoned. But the autopsy did not
bear this out. According to the doctors' report, the cause of death was
pneumonia, brought on by internal bleeding.

Despite the doctors' verdict, however, Mme de Montespan's
innocence was not generally accepted. The rumour persisted that she
had sent presents of gloves, highly scented and impregnated with
antimony, to her former rivals, and had done the same to Marie
Angélique. At that period it was fashionable for ladies of leisure,
especially the nobility, to consult fortune-tellers and 'wise-women'
who dealt in charms and love-potions, and occasionally supplied small
amounts of arsenic which, producing symptoms not unlike those
accompanying syphilis, served to curb the ardour of unruly husbands
or in desperate cases, so it was said, to quieten them for ever. Mme de
Montespan was known to have dealings with such people, and the
king could not flatly deny the charge for he himself was far from well;

94

his looks had deteriorated; he suffered from exhaustion and had headaches that might conceivably be attributed to aphrodisiacs.

In the previous year, a number of people had been arrested and accused of being poisoners. It had seemed at the beginning no more than a routine police matter; but, since some of the charges were shocking, a special Commission was set up to take evidence in secret. Little attention was given to the matter at first because it concerned persons of no importance; but suddenly, on 25 January 1680, six members of the nobility were seized, including Mazarin's niece, Olympe de Soissons (one of the king's first loves), Mme d'Alluye, her friend and a maid of honour to Queen Anne, and, most horrifying of all, the great Maréchal de Luxembourg. The two ladies immediately escaped to the Low Countries, thereby helping to confirm suspicions that the former had indeed poisoned her husband in 1673.

With such scandals in mind, it is hardly surprising that the courtiers were horrified by Marie Angélique's untimely death. The prime suspect, centre of the horrible affair, was a fortune-teller known as La Voisin, a great purveyor of love-philtres. She was tried, found guilty of being a poisoner, and executed. Nothing said at her trial implicated people of any importance; but her daughter, giving evidence after her death, swore that Mme de Montespan had been a frequent customer.

According to the police report, Mme de Montespan had been using black magic for some eight or nine years under the direction of La Voisin in order to keep the king's favour and be rid of Mlle de La Vallière. She was said to have participated in a black mass, said over her naked body, for that especial purpose. These accusations were made before the Chambre Ardente, as the secret Commission was entitled. Most of them were not proven but in general they were not out of character, considering the recklessness, cruelty and jealousy for which Athénaïs was known, and her frequent references to the devil. Mme de Sévigné, writing to her daughter at the time, said:

'My child—believe me, there are women in this world who should be stamped out, erased from the face of the earth; mark my words, they should be summarily dealt with, for perfidy, treachery, insolence and effrontery are their stock in trade, and gross dishonesty the least of their defects. They cannot boast of a single kindly impulse (I will not say loving, for that is unknown to their kind) nor even of a decent, humane or charitable one. They are fiends in human shape, with soft words and a pretty wit. They are utterly shameless. Invulnerable themselves, they delight in turning human frailty to their advantage, and gloating over their triumph. Pray put together my brief remarks; there will emerge the portrait of a certain lady who shall be nameless; would to God she were the only one of her kind.'

Mme de Montespan was not arrested. The fact of her being the mother of the king's children made it unwise to bring her to trial; but some of the charges had been horrible in the extreme, and the king was not convinced of her innocence. He was thus suddenly confronted with the probability that for the past twelve years he had given his love to a murderess, in league with the devil. Louis XIV was a man who lived in fear of God, despite his adulterous propensities, and there can be no doubt that he was profoundly shocked. Some action had to be taken, for she was dangerous and would stop at nothing, not even, perhaps, at attempting to murder him. He did not seek vengeance or publicly to disgrace her, indeed, he made her a handsome gift of money and she remained at the Court for another ten years, but although he visited her every day he took care always to be accompanied. Their love affair was finished. Thenceforward a great change came over him; he kept his sexual desires in check, and turned to the consolations of God and of Mme de Maintenon.

Persuaded by the latter, he set himself to make amends to the queen for his past adultery and unkindness, and for nearly three years became a model husband. He did not want to embark on another passionate love affair; for he was falling in love with Mme de Maintenon who, incredibly, declined to sleep with him, on the grounds that to sleep with a man who was not her husband would be sinful.

52. The king in Flanders, 1680

MOVING TO THE COUNTRY

f, after the shock of the poison trials, the king was a changed man, the effect of them on Mme de Maintenon was also profound. She had tasted power for the first time and, so she believed, had received divine confirmation of her mission to save the king. It was a task for which she felt herself not incapable, relying on God's support and his own fear of eternal damnation.

Strangely enough she had taken no active part in the downfall of Mme de Montespan. She said afterwards that had she known God's will she would have spoken out; but surely she could not have doubted that God would wish her to save the king from mortal sin. Why did she not force him to make a choice? The truth is that she loved him and lacked the courage to confront him. He needed her more and more; he was falling in love with her; he seemed unable to do without her, and that, to her, was everything. She was not physically in love with him, for that was not in her nature; but she had to an abnormal extent the instinct for maternal love, and that she lavished on the king in his loneliness and temporary misery.

The king who, according to Saint-Simon, was 'born prudent, temperate and secretive, a master of all his emotions', showed nothing of his feelings, appearing to his courtiers as calm, gracious and relaxed as was his invariable custom. Inwardly he felt the need of a change. Saint-Germain was full of ghosts and the memory of happy days never to be repeated, it was also becoming inconvenient, since there were no lodgings for the courtiers, and they constantly complained of long and tiring journeys. The king escaped more and more often to Versailles and for longer visits. He then took the great decision to move with his government and Court into the country, and to make Versailles his royal residence as soon as the rebuilding was finished.

In this he had Mme de Maintenon's entire approval. A healthy open-air life, safe from temptation by would-be mistresses, was just what he needed, and she wrote enthusiastically to the Duc du Maine's tutor, 'Versailles is astonishingly beautiful, and I am delighted to be here. The king is to give balls for us, Monsieur [The Duc d'Orléans, the King's brother] offers comedies, and we may walk wherever we please in the gardens . . . for the king wishes us all to be happy.'

99

It has often been said that the king's passion for Versailles grew out of an undying hatred of Paris and the Louvre, the result of the humiliations he had suffered there at the time of the *Frondes*, when the royal family had been forced to fly by night to the safety of Saint-Germain. Yet that theory is scarcely tenable since he had lived and held his government in Paris for the first thirty-five years of his reign. Indeed, it seems equally probable that he thought it more sensible as well as pleasanter to make a new start in fresher, less crowded surroundings, and that Versailles presented a perfect setting for regal magnificence.

Mansart's progress at the château had been spectacular; the constructional work was largely finished; Le Brun and his assistants were painting ceilings and gilding and decorating doors and walls. It was not the moment for the owner to interfere with criticisms and new ideas. Yet the king, who spent all his free time when he was not hunting inspecting the work and, on hunting-days, looked in regularly on his way home, was becoming a distinct nuisance. Mansart diverted him with supreme tact. He filled all the rooms with ladders and scaffolding so that little of the work was visible; he sent unfinished plans for the king to complete, and drawings in which glaring mistakes invited royal correction, to a chorus of praise. It did not take long for the king to lose interest, and he would escape into the gardens where, with Le Nôtre, he found more congenial occupation.

Once decided, the basic lines of Le Nôtre's grand design were never changed; but between the avenues and parterres and the great stretches of water were glades containing fountains and statues dedicated to one or other of the Greek gods or goddesses. These openings in the woods were redesigned over and over again, and there, when the château was still unready for occupation, the king and his gardener made the charming *appartements verts*, the open-air

55. The silver throne-room at Versailles, decorated under the direction of Le Brun

56. Bust of Charles Le Brun

reception-rooms with leafy walls and sunlit corridors. When summer came, courtiers could enjoy balls and concerts by the light of the moon; stroll under marble colonnades, or seek seclusion for flirtation in some hidden garden.

It was not until 6 May 1682 that Louis XIV was able to make the official announcement that thenceforward his permanent residence, the seat of his government and Court, would be the Château de Versailles, and he drove in state to take possession, accompanied by the queen, and followed by a train of ministers, prelates, courtiers, and foreign envoys. The work was far from being finished; but the king and queen's private apartments and the suite of state rooms were ready and their functions firmly established. These six magnificent rooms, the *Grand Appartement du Roi*, were named after gods and goddesses and decorated by Le Brun with stories from the legends of Greece and Rome. The finest of all was the throne-room, called, needless to say, the Salon d'Apollon, and depicting the Sun-god reigning in glory. At one end was a dais, covered with the king's famous Persian carpet woven on a gold background, on which stood the beautiful silver throne, eight feet high and of exquisite workmanship, while opposite, above the chimney-piece, hung the portrait, by Rigaud, of Louis XIV in coronation robes.

In all these rooms were displayed paintings by great masters which can now be seen in the Louvre; the walls were bright with tapestries from the factory at Les Gobelins, while against the sides stood pieces of beautiful silver furniture, designed by Le Brun, with workmanship

57. *Audience given by Louis XIV to the ambassador of the King of Spain*

so exquisite that they were estimated to form a sizable proportion of the treasures of France.

This marvellous suite of reception-rooms led to the great Hall of Mirrors, one of the most beautiful rooms in the world. Amazingly lovely by daylight, at night it was breathtaking. 'Only imagine', said one visitor, 'the effect of a hundred thousand candles in that wonderful suite of rooms. When I entered, I thought that the whole palace was on fire, for sunshine at the height of summer is not half so dazzling.'

The queen loved Versailles and was particularly delighted with her private rooms that looked south over the gardens and were full of sunlight. She was very happy in this her second honeymoon and, well aware that she owed the king's kindness to Mme de Maintenon, she gave her a copy of her latest portrait. Poor queen, her happiness did not last long, for on 30 July of the following year, 1683, she died suddenly, apparently from mistreatment by the doctors. Madame, who distrusted all doctors on principle and particularly loathed Fagon, the king's physician, was in no doubt of the cause. 'Our queen has died from an abscess beneath her arm. Instead of drawing out the pus Fagon, who unfortunately for her was her doctor, had her bled, which made the boil burst inwards . . . Immediately afterwards he dosed her with a strong emetic and, in what followed, her spirit departed for the other world. The king is very much distressed.'

He had never cared for his wife, and had made her most unhappy; but in accordance with the oath, sworn at his wedding twenty-three years earlier, he had treated her with respect and each night had shared her bed. After her death he was heard to say, 'Poor lady, this is the first sorrow that she ever caused me.' Be that as it may, he appeared more upset than truly grieved; but the effect produced was suitably mournful.

In the brief period of his unhappiness he retired (wearing violet mourning, the sign of deepest royal affliction), first to Saint-Cloud, and then to Fontainebleau. He wrote to Mme de Maintenon of his pity for the queen, and received the following reply:

'The queen is not to be pitied; she died like a saint, and now Your Majesty has a friend in heaven to pray God to forgive your sins and send you the grace which you require. Reflect, Sire, on this, and be as good a Christian as you are a great king.'

Since the death of his mother, no one had used that kind of language to Louis XIV. It gave him marvellous reassurance to hear it again from the lips of the woman with whom he was falling in love. Her 'sanctified commonsense' was one of the qualities for which he loved her so much—'as much as he was capable of loving,' said Mme de Maintenon.

The queen's death occurred at the best possible moment for that lady. 'Providence,' said Saint-Simon, 'the absolute mistress of times and circumstances, so ordained it that the queen lived long enough for his passion to reach the highest point, and not so long that it had time to cool.' A few days after the sad event he spoke frankly to Mme de Maintenon, admitting that affection had turned to love and passionate desire, which sentiments she received with her customary grave composure. She then replied so judiciously, defending her virtue on grounds of religion and purity, frightening him with thoughts of the devil and mortal sin, and thus, setting his conscience to oppose his love, she managed to achieve that incredibly high position which, Saint-Simon wrongly supposed, posterity would refuse to credit.

Although the king's heart was little affected, his life had been doubly depleted by the loss of his wife and consort. It was the first of these roles on which Mme de Maintenon's eyes were riveted; for the second she had no desire. She entered the struggle agitated, but confident in her strength, and one longs to know whether she acted to do the will of God, and save the king from damnation, or purely for her own sake because she longed for power. That will ever remain a

58. *The queen's mausoleum at St Germain des Près*

59. *The Galerie de Glaces at Versailles*

mystery since, strangely enough, her personal interests and those of the king's soul were inextricably bound together, and the charm of her piety and sweet reason that served the one purpose, served also to promote the other.

That she had before her a hard struggle Mme de Maintenon never doubted; but she went into battle trusting in God and in the king's desire for her, and immediately she succeeded. On 7 August she wrote to prevent her intractable brother from coming to her at Fontainebleau. 'The reason why I cannot see you now is so important and so wonderful that you should be filled with joy.'

On the other hand there were rumours and attacks on her character that deeply hurt her. She could not bear to be talked of as just another royal mistress, and she tried to put the matter straight in a letter, dated 15 August, to her cousin the Marquis de Villette. 'The rumour you speak of is quite untrue; the king has no mistress. You may say this without fear of appearing ill-informed.' But the gossip persisted, and she minded it so much that she threatened to retire permanently to Maintenon. 'I shall not prevent you, Madame,' said the king; 'but pray consider how your absence, even for a day, would grieve me.' He then offered to make her a duchess, but she refused, knowing the emptiness of titles. 'My entitlement to nobility in the eyes of posterity will be that I earned Your Majesty's respect. That is enough for me.'

She threatened, but she did not go, and the attacks continued with anonymous letters and cruel lampoons at her expense. She had always been generous to the poor, and she now tried to disarm scandal by good works, doubling the amount of her alms-giving, visiting the sick in a plain brown carriage, and spending much time at the charity-school she had founded at Reuil, not far from Versailles. It made no difference; but there were also voices raised in her defence by Barillon de Mortangis, the Intendant of Languedoc. 'Why heed the words of those wicked people? I have known the lady since the time when she was Mme Scarron and her very glance inspired respect. One was constantly amazed that such beauty, charm and poverty could be combined with virtue.'

She began to look ill and miserable; but by the end of September she was feeling happier, for the king had begun to form a plan to marry her in secret. He had consulted his confessor Père de La Chaise, who had written to the Pope of the king's new piety, and a letter from the Vatican had arrived, expressing the Pope's satisfaction and giving his blessing, with a present to Mme de Maintenon of the bones of Saint Candida. On 22 September she wrote to the Abbé Gobelins, 'Do not forget me in your prayers; I greatly need strength to make good use of my happiness.'

The date of the wedding is not known for certain, but is generally believed to have taken place early in the autumn of 1683, when the Court returned to Versailles, and that one night, in the king's private oratory, a mass was said during which Louis XIV and Françoise de Maintenon were married in the presence of the Archbishop of Paris and of Louvois, both of whom received the king's solemn promise never to make it public. In fact, the news was never divulged; the courtiers had no proof, yet all could see that something momentous had happened, for Mme de Maintenon became the occupant of a most luxurious suite of rooms at the top of the grand staircase, opposite the king's own apartment. Thereafter all she needed to be Queen of France was the title, and that, Madame declared, 'she was not such a fool as to demand. She knew her husband's nature and was well aware that had she made that claim she would soon have encountered ruin and disgrace.' As it was, she had everything, 'Men, ministers of state, selections, judgments, favours, all passed through her hands.' When the king worked with his ministers, she sat silently, doing embroidery in her snugly curtained niche on the other side of the fire. Sometimes he would turn to her, saying, 'Well! what does Sweet Reason think?' or, 'What is Your Solidity's opinion?' Then she would give a brief answer in her charming voice, and the discussion would proceed. But she made private arrangements to speed and ease his work, for the ministers took to calling on her when he was otherwise engaged, in order to explain the matters in question and decide the best way of presenting them. Thus for the next thirty years her influence was paramount.

She herself paid no visits and was rarely seen at the Court, except at mass in the royal chapel, when she used the queen's chair and *prie-*

60. *Madame de Maintenon*

Dieu, and in the king's coach, when she took the queen's place at his side. In private it was different, for she sat at ease in the king's presence and rose for no one but crowned heads. On the rare occasions when she wished to see the king's proud daughters, she sent for them to come to her. More often than not she wished to scold them, and they left her room in tears.

As for the king, he became increasingly happy in his second marriage. Fully understanding his bride's horror of mockery, and, above all, of losing the reputation for impregnable respectability which, all her life, she had so fiercely guarded, he treated her in public with courtly veneration, watching eagle-eyed to launch a thunderbolt at the smallest want of respect. She miraculously gave herself no airs, and he was infinitely grateful to her for the tact and perfect manners with which she saved him from all embarrassment.

Mme de Maintenon records that for three weeks after the wedding she was happy in the king's love, but that thereafter, although she continued to feel for him sisterly affection, she became increasingly fatigued by the demands he made on her. She had few illusions. She knew the king's inconstancy, and had had an unpleasant experience of the married state and 'the distasteful duties which marriage lays upon women.' 'The benefits of freedom are certain,' she said, 'and I knew them. The troubles of matrimony are equally certain, and them I did not desire.' What she seems not to have taken into account were his excessive claims on her for his marital rights, and his continual demands on her sympathy. 'When the king returns from hunting, he comes to my room,' she wrote. 'They close the doors and no one is admitted, and I have then to listen to his troubles, if he has any, and endure his moods and his ill-humour. Sometimes he weeps, for he cannot control his tears; very often he feels unwell; there is never any conversation.' She was not the only person to suffer; Madame, the king's sister-in-law, also complained that he had become a bore— 'the Great Man is positively garrulous on the subject of his soul;' and she added, 'Now that he is in love with a woman who speaks to him of nothing but penitence, he believes everything she tells him . . . and does not try to discover for himself the true meaning of religion.'

It is extraordinary to think that beneath the Sun King, that embodiment of divine majesty, there lurked a frightened little man, so fearful of his ultimate destiny that he dared not take a step without the approval of his elderly wife.

There were, however, times when her piety irritated him; he would then lose his temper and make a violent scene that reduced her to tears and left her unwell for several days. Saint-Simon says that before long she learned to appear quite seriously ill after such quarrels, and usually managed to turn them to her advantage.

One of her chief concerns, indeed, was to prevent the king from being bored with her, for then he would be likely to seek his pleasure elsewhere, perhaps with a mistress. It was therefore brilliant of her to suggest his accepting the gift of her little charity school, and becoming its patron and director. At first he was taken aback; 'No Queen of France', he said, 'ever imagined such a scheme;' but when she reminded him that her proposal was the extension of his own plan to found two cadet-schools for the sons of officers killed in the wars, he joyfully consented. He had promised, said Mme de Maintenon, to reform not only himself but the entire kingdom, and surely the religious and moral education of the future wives and mothers of his subjects deserved his royal support.

Plans for the rebuilding and enlargement of the school became an absorbing hobby and a shared pleasure. Within the year (1684) he had bought and renovated the derelict château on which Mme de Maintenon had her eye, and had constructed there the famous Maison Royale de Saint-Cyr, where two hundred and fifty girls of gentle birth were to be brought up in the odour of sanctity, but 'free from the pettiness and triviality of convents.' 'I have many convents in my kingdom,' he said, 'and I do not intend to establish another. I venture to think that ladies with a knowledge of the world are better fitted than nuns to educate young ladies who are destined to live in the world.'

It delighted him to find that he and his wife could work together, and that Françoise shared his conviction that great enterprises are bound to succeed if the details are carefully enough considered. They discussed every aspect. 'What dismal little bonnets!' he exclaimed on seeing the proposed uniforms, and he had them redesigned to show off pretty curls. On the same excuse, he changed the colour of the gloves from black to bronze, saying that funeral black was altogether too gloomy. Mme de Maintenon was in her element at the school. She was a born governess; but it should never be forgotten that even in these later years she had many charms. Much of her beauty still remained; she had a gentle flute-like voice, and although at first sight she might look severe, a sudden radiant smile would warm and illuminate her whole face; moreover, when she spoke, she had a turn of phrase that made her words appear delightfully comic. Children loved her, and she loved children. All her life she enjoyed their company, and her house was never without them.

As for the king, it was one of his most endearing qualities that he, too, was genuinely fond of children. He took the deepest interest in Saint-Cyr, and went every week to hear the little ones say their lessons, and read to them with the youngest on his knee. There was nothing about him then of terrifying majesty; he was kind and gentle, no one was afraid of him, and both the dames and their pupils looked forward to his visits.

Sometimes he would fetch Mme de Maintenon from the school and drive back with her to Versailles, and the notes he wrote to forewarn her are still in existence. 'If you will give me time to change my coat, I think that I can come to Compline, at Saint-Cyr, and bring you home in my carriage. If this plan pleases you, choose some ladies to accompany us, and let me know that you consent.'

'I have changed my plans. I shall hunt today and afterwards come to the gates of Saint-Cyr, on the park side, where my coach will be waiting. I hope you will join me there with such ladies as you please to invite, and we will go for a drive in the park. Tomorrow, returning from Saint-Germain, I shall be decently dressed and able to come to Compline in the chapel. Then we can return together. Send me word if you will join me at the park gates, or whether you would prefer the coach to take you up in the courtyard of Saint-Cyr.'

These little notes, treasured by the dames of Saint-Cyr, are almost all that remains of Louis XIV's correspondence with Mme de Maintenon; the rest she burned after his death. They serve to show how cosy and happy they were together at this period; a few years later, when Saint-Cyr was established and flourishing, there was terrible trouble at the school.

Fénelon, the Archbishop of Cambrai and tutor of the king's grandsons, was at that time Mme de Maintenon's spiritual director. He brought to her notice with the strongest recommendation a saintly lady, named Mme Guyon, who was a Quietist, preaching of pure love and grace descending into the souls of the elect. She had also written a book, *A Short and Easy Way to Prayer from the Heart*, which so pleased Mme de Maintenon that she invited Mme Guyon to stay at the school

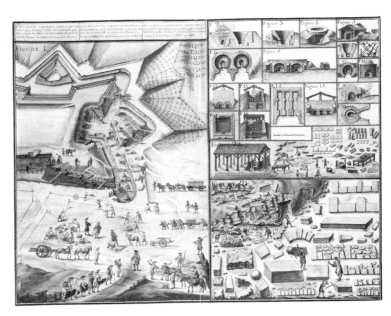

61. *Two pages from Masse's famous Atlas*, Traité de l'Attaque

and lecture to the girls, as a result of which they began to hear voices, practised 'going into ecstasy', and became much addicted to swooning. Mme de Maintenon, seriously alarmed, listened to her confessor's warning against 'extreme forms of doctrine that come dangerously near to heresy', and sent Mme Guyon packing; but worse was to come. Fénelon sprang to the defence of his protégée with a book entitled *Explanation of the Maxims of the Saints Regarding the Life of the Soul*; this was followed by two volumes from Bossuet, the Bishop of Meaux, giving a very different version of the affair. Other prelates wrote books, and famous preachers made fashionable churches ring with cries of heresy. Soon the great churchmen of France were at each other's throats, and there appeared real danger of a schism.

The king, furiously angry, turned his rage upon Mme de Maintenon for having patronized and brought forward Mme Guyon, and for her complicity with Fénelon whom he profoundly distrusted. There was a terrible scene in which he furiously accused her of causing the disturbance, and thereafter, for several weeks, refused to see her. 'Never', she wrote to the dames of Saint-Cyr, 'have I been so near to disgrace. What will become of me in my affliction? I beseech you to pray for me.' She took to her bed and made herself ill with weeping; but the king did not relent until his confessor told him that his cruelty might be the death of her. Then he did visit her, and sitting by her bed took her hand, saying very gently, 'Madame, are you going to die of this affair?' Whereupon they made it up, and never again (that one knows of) had a serious quarrel.

62. Louis XIV in armour

DULL DAYS AT VERSAILLES

ne effect of Louis XIV's second marriage had been to make the change in him apparent to all. The Archbishop of Sens recorded that 'the slow and hesitant change in the king's demeanour and conduct became more clearly marked in the years 1683–1684. He thereafter ceased to disguise his new-found piety, and no longer feared to show his true nature, replacing with devoted practice of his religious duties the amorous affairs that had hitherto absorbed him.'

If anyone at the Court still retained doubts of the king's second marriage, it was not the archbishop. 'I can bear witness', he said, 'that the king and Mme de Maintenon went through a genuine marriage ceremony, blessed by the Church,' and he produced evidence which he found entirely convincing. Firstly, that no one but a wife, on those occasions when age or infirmity obliged her to retire early, would undress and get into bed in the very room where the king worked with his ministers. Secondly, that the king would not otherwise have said to his brother, when Monsieur entered his room to find him in bed and most scantily attired, with Mme de Maintenon sitting beside him, 'You will readily perceive, brother, from my state of undress, what my relationship is to Mme de Maintenon.'

The constraints of respectability that so often destroy marital bliss had the opposite effect on Louis XIV. In the first three years after his wedding he was as happy as he had ever been before. He was middle-aged and still in good health. Hard work, hard exercise out hunting and in his garden, and the comfort of tranquil love suited his constitution while, thanks to his wife's spritual nursing, his conscience was quiet and his mind at peace.

Her power over him lay essentially in matters of religion and morality. Under her influence he took to carrying a prayer-book and a rosary in his pocket, and might be seen, in church, telling his beads with the utmost reverence. He never missed mass or fast-days unless suffering from some real indisposition and, in the opinion of his courtiers, became excessively particular regarding their behaviour in church, taking note of absences, and looking very black indeed at the least noise or sound of whispering. All this was sincere, yet his

confessor accused him of having no understanding of religion; and
Fénelon wrote to Mme de Maintenon, 'the king has no sense of the
true meaning of his religious duties.' She, who fervently believed that
God had charged her personally with his soul's salvation, prayed
every morning, 'Oh! Lord, thou hast placed me where I am. Oh! thou
who holdest in thy hand the hearts of kings, open this king's heart to
me that I may put into it the good which thou desirest.'

She did not find life with the king agreeable; but she soon laid
down rules that made it at least bearable. She would not travel with
him in his coach; the speed of his galloping horses made the jolting a
torment; the draught through the open windows; the dust and dirt
thrown up by the hooves of the mounted escort, and the king's
constant proffering of cakes and sweets, made long journeys with him
disagreeable and most exhausting. She travelled quietly in her own
unpretentious carriage, accompanied by one or two ladies; but
whether their destination was Fontainebleau, Compiègne or to his
army's headquarters, she was always there before him, waiting to
receive him, sitting quietly with her needlework in a room filled with
flowers and cheerful company.

Every morning at Versailles she was up by seven, giving audiences to the clergy or to ministers. Very occasionally, she visited the
ministers for war and finance in their own apartments. At eight
o'clock she drove to Saint-Cyr, and there arrived helped to make the
youngest children ready for their lessons, brushing their hair and
talking to them, so that she got to know them individually and could
help them in any troubles. She then retired to her warm and comfortable bed in her private flat and busied herself with the running of
the school, and also of the clergy, for being constantly consulted by
prelates who desired her to influence the king, she had begun, says
Saint-Simon, to regard herself as a mother of the church, with a duty
to praise or reprimand, but most frequently the latter.

63. Louis XIV
playing billiards in the
third chamber

64. Louis XIV dancing at Versailles

The king did not forget his promise to make life at Versailles pleasant for his courtiers. Three days a week, on Mondays, Wednesdays and Fridays, from six until ten o'clock, he held '*Appartement*', an evening reception in the *Galerie des Glaces* and the splendid suite of state-rooms. During those four hours etiquette was relaxed, chairs were brought for the ladies, and the king moved among his guests like a genial host, chatting with them and seeing to their comfort. The pleasures provided were refreshments, a collation with the immense pyramidal arrangements of exotic fruit that were then in fashion, billiards, dancing, a concert, and card-tables for gambling. No one was required to rise when princes and princesses of the Blood passed through the rooms.

The *Galerie des Glaces* and the other state-rooms were fully illuminated with tens of thousands of candles, the great mirrors reflected dazzling jewels and beautiful dresses. Not only courtiers and the nobility were invited, but poets, dramatists, painters, men of letters and distinguished foreigners. Those were the times when intrigues were hatched and love affairs made swift progress. But the courtiers were not greatly exhilarated; there were no state balls and no splendid fêtes in prospect; 'Always the same diversions, the same hours, the same people,' moaned one disgruntled lady. Even the king had lost his appetite for pleasure; only hunting and billiards amused him, and the only plays he cared to see were occasional religious dramas written by Racine for performance by the schoolgirls of Saint-Cyr. The Italian players, who had been considered so very funny, were peremptorily banished after *The Sham Prude*, a comedy that pointed rather too clearly at Mme de Maintenon.

Versailles, once famous for its magnificent fêtes, would have been thought very dull had it not been for the gambling. '*Appartement*' was a somewhat staid entertainment; but in the card-rooms, where the nobility played for high stakes, good manners and dignity were not insisted upon. Losers shrieked and howled and flung themselves off their chairs when the turn of a card cost them their whole fortunes. They also cheated, when they could do so unobserved; indeed, the Marquis de Dangeau and the Marquise de Soissons who won by skill and fair means were especially admired, and considered astonishing.

It would be a great mistake to think of Versailles as a private palace built by Louis XIV solely for his own pleasure and that of his courtiers. On the days when there was no '*Appartement*' the beautiful *Galerie des Glaces* and the *Grand Appartement* were both open to the public, who came to see the king on his way to mass and look at the art collections that made Versailles the finest museum in Europe. A public coach-service arrived twice a day from Paris, bringing sightseers to the golden gate for twenty-five sous each. All that was required of visitors was to be decently attired; the swords that fashion demanded could be hired at the entrance, and the public were not only allowed into the state-rooms and gardens, but might join with the courtiers and watch the king and his family eating their supper.

They came in crowds—'Monkeys and rabbits', wrote one memoirist, 'stepped down at the château gates, wiped the dust from their shoes, buckled on hired swords, entered the Great Gallery and, at their leisure, gazed on the royal family, commenting on the bearing and appearance of the princesses. They then played at being courtiers for as long as they pleased, took up their position between two dukes, and rubbed shoulders with princes. After that, nothing prevented the monkeys and rabbits from appearing at the king's dinner as though they were members of the Court.'

Another writer describing the scene says, 'It is hard to conceive the kind of mob that descended upon the *Galerie des Glaces*. Among the six thousand admitted there might well have been spies and brigands. There was no discrimination. On visiting days, the *Grand Appartement* resembled a fair or a market-place, with the same smells and heat. On some days the crowds were so big in the gardens that the king was prevented from taking his daily exercise.'

Louis XIV was no longer pouring vast sums into Versailles; but, feeling he needed a bolt-hole, an escape from the crowds, he decided to rebuild Trianon, the little house he had made for Mme de Montespan. It was to be a retreat for himself and Mme de Maintenon, where they could enjoy peace, quiet and solitude in a garden full of sweet-scented flowers. In 1687 he therefore ordered Mansart to demolish the old

Trianon de Porcelaine, so called because of the blue and white tiles that covered the façade, and to build the Marble Trianon on the same spot. The work was to proceed at the greatest possible speed, and to be finished in two years' time at the latest. In order to expedite matters, the king had a tent pitched on the site in the summer of 1688, and slept there, so as to be able to inspect the work each morning before breakfast and urge on the workmen.

Mme de Maintenon, who thought that enough had been spent on Versailles, was none the less in favour of rebuilding the little house, though if she imagined, like Louise de La Vallière, that the king had an inclination for love in a cottage and the simple life, she was doomed to be disappointed. Louis XIV's idea was different. He wanted a miniature Versailles, with state-rooms leading one out of another, terraces, marble colonnades, fountains, and canals; above all, he wanted a flower-garden. Money was once more of no account; huge fortunes were spent on machines to bring water to the site, and although the budget for building works had been reduced in the past two years, thousands of extra workmen and horses were hired to labour in the garden.

66. The Grand Trianon

Whatever the cost, the result was a delight. A profusion of flowers was planted to scent the air beneath Mme de Maintenon's windows. Indeed, Le Nôtre recorded that two million flowerpots were kept in constant use throughout the whole season, and the old gardener, who would not allow flowerbeds to spoil the austerity of his formal gardens around the château, became lyrical about those at Trianon. 'You never see a dead leaf there or a shrub out of bloom . . . There are groups of trees, interspersed by narrow waterways that wind their way haphazard, twisting and turning through the clearings and around the groves, with fountains placed irregularly here and there. It is a place for ladies to come to with their sewing and other employments, and to enjoy a picnic in the open air.'

But Trianon, when it was finished, turned out to be too small, and too near the château to provide the peace and rest that the king felt he needed. Just as thirty years earlier he had made Versailles as an escape from the crowds of Paris and the perpetual demands of courtiers, he now built Marly as a holiday house, where he could invite his friends for short visits, with the constraints of etiquette completely relaxed. 'Hats, gentlemen!' he would be able to say, and his guests would be free to wear their hats in his presence, and go off to enjoy their holiday wherever the fancy took them, among the pleasures which he had provided.

As the years passed, Louis XIV's magnificent health began to cause concern. He was becoming exhausted with work. Colbert and Louvois, his two outstandingly brilliant ministers, died in 1683 and 1691 respectively and, instead of replacing them, the king took over the direction of both their ministries. Taught to believe in his own infallibility in statecraft, he felt fully capable of personally administering the departments of war and finance until such time as he had trained younger men to undertake them. Meanwhile, he did the work himself.

From eight o'clock until twelve each morning he held councils or gave audience to marshals or ambassadors. After mass, at midday, and his dinner in public, he went out for exercise, hunting or shooting on three days of the working-week and on the other two walking in his gardens or making excursions to Trianon or Clagny. From four until six was his private time, behind locked doors, with Mme de Maintenon; then the doors were opened and he resumed work. Hour after hour the old couple sat together on either side of the fireplace, she silently knitting for the poor or embroidering for her school, he conferring with one or other of his ministers, studying dispatches, dictating letters. At ten o'clock he went to supper with the princesses, appearing to the Court for the briefest possible moment when there

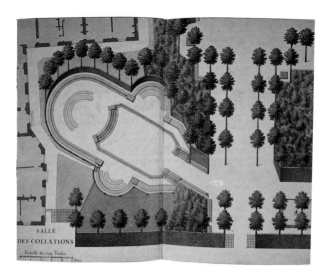

*67. A design for
the gardens at
Marly*

SALLE
DES COLLATIONS
Echelle de cinq Toises.

was '*Appartement*', and very soon afterwards retiring to his study to
deal, until far into the night, with the day's enormous mail.

He made some bad mistakes. The early aggressive wars in Flanders
and the Netherlands had been supremely successful. The French
armies had appeared invincible, and the military glory of the Sun King
reached its summit. Europe was dazzled by the rays of his splendour,
and the beauties of Versailles were the admiration of every foreign
Court. The third war, begun in 1688, was less well-judged. It dragged
on for nine years, until 1697, and, although the French armies won
many victories, proved terribly costly in lives and financially ruinous.
A worse error was the revocation of the Edict of Nantes, by which, in
1598, Henri IV had brought peace to France after the religious wars.
Encouraged by the orthodox clergy and with the approval of most of
his subjects King Louis sent a regiment of dragoons to force 'conversion' upon the French Protestants. There then ensued the brutal
raids, known as the *dragonnades*, in which French soldiers tortured and
killed the Huguenots, their Protestant fellow-countrymen, in an
attempt to persuade them to a mass conversion. At last, on 17 October
1685 the Edict was revoked and the practice of the Protestant religion forbidden in France by law. As a result, nearly half a million
Huguenots were driven into exile, leaving the army and the navy
much depleted and French industry the poorer by thousands of its
most highly skilled craftsmen.

The king was said to have been largely unaware of the cruelties
involved. Indeed, he had expressly forbidden violence, and the blame
was laid chiefly on Marsillac, a brutal and ambitious intendant in
command of the dragoons. But there is no doubt that in the eyes of the
Catholic clergy, the end justified the cruel means. 'Let us spread word

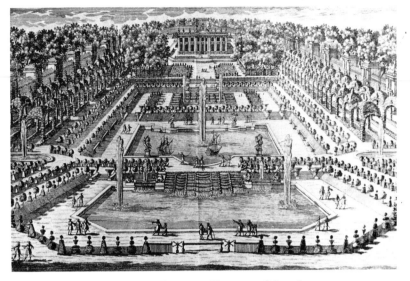

68. General view of Marly

of this modern miracle,' said Bossuet, 'and sing to Heaven of the piety of King Louis. Let us lift up our hearts to God, and tell this new Constantine, this modern Charlemagne, "What you have done is worthy of your reign; for, by your deed, there is no more heresy."' Most of the French people (Protestants apart) heartily approved the Revocation. Mme de Sévigné wrote, 'Nothing is as beautiful as that which it contains; and no king has ever done, or ever will do, a deed more memorable.' Voltaire was not of that opinion. He called the Revocation 'one of the greatest disasters that ever afflicted France'.

But the ultimate mistake that brought France close to collapse and shattered for ever the Sun King's military glory was the decision, in 1700, to accept intact the inheritance of the throne of Spain and the mighty Spanish Empire. This violation of Louis XIV's signed undertaking in two Treaties of Partition was the cause of the War of the Spanish Succession, in which France stood alone against the united armies of Austria, England and the Netherlands, and suffered, in 1704, 1706 and 1708, the successive defeats of Blenheim, Ramillies and Oudenarde. By 1709 the country was near starvation, and the economy in ruins.

Meanwhile, at Versailles, the Court sank into a gloomy appearance of pious respectability, although the Duchesse d'Orléans wrote to her aunt that the fashion for wearing huge diamond crosses had no real religious significance. Taxes rose, new levies were introduced, and although it was the poor who suffered most, nearly all of the courtiers at Versailles were in financial difficulties. Money-making, not pleasure, became their chief interest; most of their days, and nights also, were spent at the card-tables, playing for stakes they could not afford, and Madame wrote of 'tragic events for which the game of lansquenet is responsible'. The royal family lost fortunes and the king

69. The water pumping machine at Marly

paid their debts without complaint. He liked his courtiers to be dependent on his bounty, and went so far as to tell his children that he expected them to lose money at cards.

In the course of time Versailles dwindled into being little better than a money-market. The courtiers charged fees for every kind of service, for recommendations likely to lead to jobs; for introductions; for good places from which to catch the king's eye as he walked to mass; for tickets and invitations. It was all done quite openly; for example, Mme de Montauban, anxious to go to Marly, offered the Princesse d'Harcourt a thousand écus to gain the king's consent. 'It seems, Sire,' said that lady to the king, 'that Mme de Montauban has never yet been to Marly.' 'I am well aware of that,' replied His Majesty. 'Yet she would, I think, much like to go.' 'I do not doubt it, Madame.' 'Then, Sire, will Your Majesty not deign to name her?' 'I think it unnecessary, Madame.' 'But Sire, it is worth a thousand écus to me, and Your Majesty knows that I sorely need the money.'

In 1686, the king's failing health deteriorated so rapidly and he suffered so much pain that the doctors decided to take action. The cause, at first, was not evident, and when the truth was discovered it was kept secret for several months because the nature of the malady (an anal fistula) was considered indelicate and required an agonizing operation. During that interval, Felix, the king's surgeon, practised on poor patients in the Paris hospitals until he felt supremely competent, and at last, at eight o'clock on the morning of 16 November, *La Grande Opération* was performed. The king bore the terrible pain with exemplary patience. He spoke only once, towards the end, when he said to the doctors, 'Messieurs, are you nearly done? Go on with your work and do not treat me as a king. I desire you to allow me to recover as though I were a peasant.' That same evening he received visits and held council, even although, according to the Abbé de Choisy, 'Pain was written on his face, and his forehead was bathed in sweat.' Thereafter he insisted on having his courtiers admitted twice a day, at his mealtimes, to his bedroom, in order to show them that he was recovering. 'We are not private persons,' he said, 'we belong to our people.'

The operation was completely successful; the wound healed, and the king returned to his normal life of work, hunting, gardening, and the calm society of Mme de Maintenon, who had cared devotedly for him during his illness but not to the extent of diverting her whole attention from Saint-Cyr. As he regained his energies it became apparent that a life of pious austerity did not wholly suit him; she became seriously alarmed lest he revert to thoughts of taking a mistress, and showed her disapproval of his invitations to elderly ladies to visit him on rainy afternoons. Such visits were purely social occasions for the pleasure of good conversation in the old style of the '*Précieuses*', yet the ladies were taken to his study by the back way and, when bursts of laughter were heard through the closed doors, Mme de Maintenon felt far from easy. There was no cause for her to be alarmed: the king had had enough of passionate love and was well content with the physical side of his marriage—far too much so his old wife thought. Indeed, she had written to her spiritual director complaining of 'those painful occasions' to which she was daily subjected, but he had replied that she should consider it 'an especial grace to do from pure virtue what many other women do for pleasure or profit'. She served God, he continued, by keeping His Majesty from sin, and should turn her thoughts to Heaven, 'where the perturbations of this life no longer exist.'

Mme de Maintenon resigned herself to her duties, but complained bitterly in letters to her friends of the trials of her life and the deceptive glamour of royal palaces. She lectured the older girls at Saint-Cyr on the few pleasures and many pains of married life, and the folly of envying life at the Court, which offered nothing but strife, exhaustion and discomfort. In that respect Versailles, in all probability, was not greatly changed; but it was certainly wanting in gaiety. There were no more festivities and when darkness fell gloom descended, for to save money only half the candles were lit in the chandeliers, and in the passages there were no lights at all.

The king himself, though much against his will, felt constrained to set the example in economy. He launched an appeal to the nobility and gentry to send their silver plate to the mint to be melted down for cash, and made a personal contribution of much of the silver furniture in the *Galerie des Glaces* and the state apartments. Even the great silver throne was sacrificed and the silver balustrade in the throne room, regardless of the beautiful craftsmanship, worth far more, in terms of money, than the weight of the silver itself. The response was not overwhelming; many of the richer families sent silver of inferior quality and kept the best; but it became the fashion to buy porcelain, and before long the entire Court was said to be 'eating off china'.

All of this combined to depress the king, who loved above all good cheer and happiness. Madame wrote that he 'was visibly aging and was becoming fat and looking like an old man'. He may have felt something of the kind himself for he made abortive attempts at jollity with the younger members of his family—his three grandsons, the Dukes of Bourgogne, Anjou, and Berry, who were respectively seven, six, and three years old, and the three legitimated princesses, daughters of Louise de La Vallière and Athénaïs de Montespan. They were all terrified of him and scarcely dared to speak in his presence; thus when he put aside his immense dignity to throw bread pills at supper, or start a competition in spitting olive stones, there was very little laughter.

As the princesses grew up, they quarrelled and created scandals; the two youngest especially were drunk more often than they were sober, and conducted their love affairs in a way that shocked respectable ladies. Mme de Maintenon was frequently called upon to deliver reprimands, particularly when they were caught smoking, a habit which the king considered hateful in young women. The princesses visited her room as rarely as possible, and Saint-Simon noticed that when they emerged they were most often in floods of tears.

At one time Mme de Maintenon believed that the Princesse de Conti, Louise de La Vallière's daughter, might gain the king's affection and give him the kind of family love which he so much needed. Unfortunately the princess had the imprudence to post a private letter by the ordinary mail which was intercepted and sent to the king. It contained mocking references to Mme de Maintenon and his marriage to her, and thus provoked a terrible scene, destroying any hope of establishing a warm relationship.

Quite unexpectedly, however, everything changed with the arrival at Versailles of a child of ten, a charming little girl who was to become

the Duchesse de Bourgogne, and whose sweetness and high spirits made even Mme de Maintenon smile. As for the king, he immediately fell in love; she became his boon companion, his pet and playfellow, who lightened his life and transformed the entire Court by her gaiety.

71. The Duc de Bourgogne

MARIE ADELAIDE OF SAVOY

I n 1696, Louis XIV signed a peace treaty with the Duke of Savoy, the chief clause of which concerned the marriage of the latter's daughter Marie Adelaide to the twelve-year-old Duc de Bourgogne, the king's eldest grandson, heir presumptive after the Grand Dauphin's death to the throne of France. For a king so powerful and glory-loving to have sought a future Queen of France in the poverty-stricken little duchy of Savoy may have seemed extraordinary; but France needed peace, and Savoy had a geographical importance altogether out of proportion to its diminutive size. The duke's dominion covered both sides of the Alpine passes that led into Italy, and commanded the roads which the armies of France and Austria both needed to use in every campaign. The friendship of the Duke of Savoy was thus invaluable, for he could assist or prevent the passage of troops, as best served his personal interests. It was worth paying a high price to secure him for an ally.

Unfortunately, Victor Amadeus, the duke in question, was an unreliable character, to whom loyalty in an alliance meant nothing. He had a scandalous reputation for changing sides in war, whenever his immediate advantage suggested such a course, and had been known to do so twice in the course of a single campaign. In 1696, however, both the king and the duke were eager to make peace. Louis XIV offered generous compensation for damages inflicted on Savoy during the war: the restitution of Nice and other territory captured, the recognition of the duke's royal status and his claim to be greeted with royal salutes and addressed as a Royal Highness. But of all the clauses in the treaty, the most binding was held to be the marriage of the little princess to the Duc de Bourgogne. Her father was known to be extremely fond of her; she was not yet of an age for marriage, being only ten years old, and so would go to France to be educated and trained as a future queen. It was hoped that he would regard her as a kind of hostage, and be true to his new alliance for the sake of her happiness. But such considerations were not in the duke's nature. When, eight years later, the armies of France began to suffer a series of humiliating defeats, he soon returned to alliance with Austria.

The motives for the betrothal at the time, however, were well calculated. In terms of wealth and power Adelaide of Savoy may have been insignificant, but her birth was impeccable. Her mother had been a French princess, the daughter of Monsieur (the king's brother) by his first wife, the lovely and irresistibly charming Henrietta of England, with whom Louis XIV had been dangerously in love until Louise de La Vallière swept him off his feet. Her paternal grandmother, known as Madame Royale, was also French by birth, and nine years younger than the king. She had been brought up at the French Court and had known Versailles in the great days when King Louis was young, and love and pleasure were the order of the day. Her palace at Turin was a reflection of Saint-Germain and the beauty of Versailles, and she surrounded herself with the liveliest and most lovely young girls that the duchy could provide. A fascinating and still a beautiful woman, she loved the society of young people. All the brilliance and gaiety of Savoy were to be found in her drawing-rooms; laughter was heard there all day and far into the night, when dancing gave place to games like blind man's buff, in which etiquette was relaxed to an astonishing degree.

Madame Royale and Adelaide's mother, Duchess Anne, combined, as soon as the betrothal became a certainty, to fill the little girl's mind with the joys she would find at Versailles, the most exciting, most beautiful place on earth, as they truly believed. Her father, meanwhile, took charge of her training to become a French princess. He made her understand her bounden duty to reverence the king in his awesome majesty, and give essential support to his appalling responsibility as the absolute lord and master under God, of twenty millions of French men and women. In public, at all times she must think of this and conduct herself in his presence with awed respect. In private it would be different; then she could be herself, for the king was her kind old uncle who loved children and enjoyed playing with them. All that he would want from her was to love him and be happy.

He had married, her parents told her, a sweet lady, who was his wife, but not the queen. She also loved children and Adelaide, who was to be her special care, might call her 'Aunt'. If Adelaide would return her love and always follow her advice, she could not fail to do right. By such instruction, said Saint-Simon, her wise parents showed her the only way to be happy at the Court of France.

The little princess was a light-hearted, merry child, with an affectionate, trustful nature. She loved her family, especially Madame Royale her grandmother, and accepted without question all that they told her of her future happiness. Thus, when she cried at the thought of leaving home she was able to comfort herself and recover her spirits in the conviction that she would be loved in her new country and

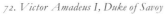
72. *Victor Amadeus I, Duke of Savoy*

73. *Christine, wife of Victor Amadeus I*

enjoy the glory of learning to be its queen. In the event, she was not to be disappointed.

Meanwhile, the king and Mme de Maintenon looked forward to her arrival with high hopes and some trepidation. The child was of the very highest importance, and so was their task of training her for her future position. She would be a mutual interest, their pet and pupil; Mme de Maintenon should supervise her religious instruction, schooling and behaviour, the king impart such rudiments of statecraft as she could imbibe, and plan her amusements.

Mme de Maintenon was more than a little perturbed when letters arrived from the French ladies accompanying Adelaide on the long journey from Italy to Fontainebleau, where the Court was in residence. These favoured ladies of her new household spoke of nothing but her witty remarks, her tirelessness, and the clever way in which she had intervened to finish the speech of a tongue-tied official. It all sounded too much like smartness and chatter to Mme de Maintenon, and she had enough of that already from the clever, malicious children of Mme de Montespan. Her hopes faded of Adelaide's becoming the king's darling, a delightful hobby for them both to share, and she was gripped by the fear that disappointment might lead him to seek elsewhere, perhaps in a mistress, an object on which to lavish his

74. *The Duc de Saint-Simon*

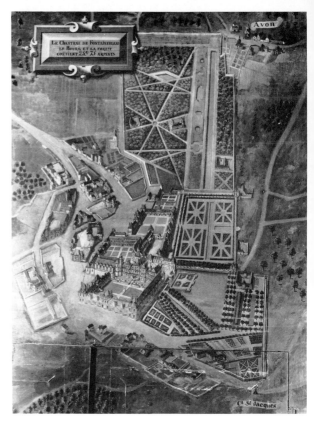

75. *An early bird's-eye
view of Fontainebleau*

affection. Where then would be her religious purpose, her mission to save his soul?

As for the king, he was not pleased by the reports, but his hopes were not dashed. Perhaps he remembered Henrietta, her adorable grandmother, and did not wish to believe that Adelaide would fail him. However that may have been, his excitement rose to such a pitch that the Comte de Govion, the Duke of Savoy's ambassador, reported to his master that the king's impatience to see the princess was quite incomprehensible. He talked unceasingly about her, and even interrupted meetings of the Council to repeat, with pride and many embellishments, her little impromptu speeches which he found so moving.

All of this took place at Fontainebleau, where etiquette required him to await her arrival. But at the last minute, regardless of the rules, he went all the way to Montargis to meet her, so as to be the first to greet her on the soil of France. It was a case of love at first sight.

The following letter to Mme de Maintenon, almost the only letter she did not burn immediately after his death, tells of his delight:

'I reached here shortly after four o'clock; but the princess did not appear until nearly six. I went out to receive her at the door of her coach. She waited for me to speak, and then replied exceedingly well, with just a trace of shyness that would very much have pleased you. I took her by the hand and led her through the crowd and up to her room, from time to time making them shine the torchlight upon her face so that people might see her. She bore the walk and the lights bravely and modestly, and at last we reached her room, where the heat and crush were enough to kill one. Now and again I presented the people nearest us, and I watched her closely so as to give you my impressions.'

He went on to say that she had the most graceful and the prettiest figure imaginable, that she was dressed 'fit to be painted, that her eyes were bright and beautiful and her complexion perfect. She has', he continued, 'masses of fair hair, a wide red mouth, and long, white irregular teeth.' [They later turned black, causing her agonizing pain.] 'Her hands are rather red, as little girls' hands so often are. She does not say much so far as I have observed; but she does not become embarrassed when people stare at her, and behaves altogether like a woman of the world. Her curtsey is not at all good, rather after the Italian manner; indeed, there is something Italian about her face; but she is very pleasing; I could see that in everyone's eyes . . . Speaking as I always do to you, I can truly say that I found her all that could be desired; I should even be sorry if she were better-looking.

'To sum up, I find her absolutely perfect, save only for her curtsey.* As for me, I have done marvels up to now. I only hope I can sustain the easy manner† which I have adopted until we reach Fontainebleau.'

They rose at six next morning; the king sat beside her as they finished dressing her and brushed her hair, and at nine o'clock they processed to church in state, through a crowd of twenty thousand people. Her behaviour at the service was exemplary, which the king noticed with relieved approval, and she had her first sight of the great Louis XIV in majesty, when the entire congregation turned their backs on God's altar in order to salute His lieutenant upon earth.

It was a long, slow journey to Fontainebleau, taking five hours in Adelaide's heavy coach, in contrast to the king's two-and-a-half hour gallop to Montargis on the previous day. Arrived at the palace, at four in the afternoon, they found the great courtyard full to overflowing with a host of courtiers, attended by their retinues and servants, crowding outside in the gathering darkness of a November evening to catch the first glimpse of their future queen. Adelaide showed no sign

*A graceful curtsey was a sign of good breeding. To be clumsy was considered vulgar.
†The king, well aware that his bearing and manner were so awe-inspiring that strangers were frequently struck dumb in his presence, was determined not to frighten Adelaide.

76. Marie Adelaide of Savoy

of being tired, though after so long and exciting a day she might well have been tearful and exhausted. She was, at any rate, not allowed to be either, for the king, in what Sainte-Beuve calls 'his monumental and hideous selfishness', does not seem to have given her a thought. He himself went off to rest and chat with Mme de Maintenon after handing the little princess over to his brother to receive presentations, and for two long hours she stood in her heavy dress, curtseying, smiling, saying now and then a gracious word. Tired she may have been, but there was no fault to be found with her performance, for even the carping Duc de Saint-Simon had no blame to utter. The courtiers, moved by her patient endurance and desire to please, called her *franc du collier*, a willing horse, and loved her for her readiness to do her duty.

At last the presentations came to an end, and Adelaide was allowed to go to her room, take off her stiff Court dress, and eat her supper; but she was still allowed no rest. Soon after she had finished, both sides of the great double doors were opened and the king appeared, leading his wife by the hand for the formal presentation. He did not stay long, but left them together for Mme de Maintenon to form her own judgement. It was, for the latter, the great moment on which she thought her whole future depended, and she looked into the child's sparkling black eyes, fearing to see a glint of malice or ambition. She need not have worried, there was nothing in them to cause her anxiety, and, like the king, she was immediately bowled over by Adelaide's captivating charm. Next day, she wrote to Duchess Anne, in Savoy:

'Your daughter has a natural courtesy that makes her incapable of saying anything but what is pleasing. I tried yesterday to prevent her from kissing me, saying that I was too old. "Oh no! not at all too old for kisses," she replied, and when the king had left the room, she did me the honour to put her arms round me and embrace me. Then she made me sit down, having very quickly noticed that I could not stand for long, and, settling down with a most charming smile, almost in my lap, she said, "Mamma has told me to give you her dear love, and to ask you to love me. Pray teach me what I should do so as to please the king." Those, Madame, are her very words, but how describe the merry look that accompanied them!'

Nearly everyone fell in love with Adelaide. The Duc de Saint-Simon says that 'she loved to be pleasing, even to the most ordinary and commonplace people, but seemed never to court popularity. When you were with her, you were tempted to believe that she was wholly and solely your friend. The entire Court was enlivened by her gaiety and high spirits; she flitted hither and thither like a nymph, like a summer breeze, bringing life and merriment wherever she passed.

Every entertainment was graced by her presence, for she was the life and soul of all the balls and plays and fêtes, besides enchanting everyone with the elegance and neatness of her dancing.'

She was indeed 'like a breath of spring', playing every game, from spillikins to blind-man's buff, with enthusiasm, laughing, singing, dancing on her chair at meals to the horror of Nanon, Mme de Maintenon's confidential maid, who filled the post of Nanny. Only when she had bouts of toothache did her spirits flag; otherwise she never admitted to feeling unwell, was never tired, never had a cold, never sought an excuse to stay at home or avoid the king's company. She found in him, as her mother had promised, a kind old uncle who warmed her with his love and who needed her affection. She was, it seems, quite unafraid, calling him 'tu' in private, climbing on his knee, ruffling his hair, opening his letters, and using the kind of 'baby-talk' in a mixture of French and Italian, which he found marvellously amusing.

The king who, in 1696, was fifty-eight years old (Mme de Maintenon was sixty-one), gave his whole heart to Adelaide, as though she had been his own little daughter, and never, since the early days with Louise de La Vallière, had he been so happy. She went out with him every afternoon and before long did not wait for his summons, but at two o'clock went running down the *Galerie des Glaces* and into his study without knocking, regardless of the rules. From her he enjoyed the impertinence, and rising with a comically rueful smile to the minister with whom he was working, he allowed her to lead him, chattering, down the great staircase and out to explore the gardens, followed by a pretty pony-carriage in case she should be tired.

She listened intently while he told her tales of the Greek gods and goddesses among the statues; shrieked with delight on the children's mountain-railway as it hurtled down the slopes in the park. Together they fed the ducks, rowed boats on the canal, and looked at the wild beasts in the menagerie, which he gave her as a present, for her very own, to do with as she pleased. Nothing could have delighted her more; she turned the central building into a replica of her mother's house in Savoy, with a dairy, still-room, kitchen and sewing-room, where she and her friends made butter and cheese, jams, and all manner of delicious cakes for the king's own eating. The king did still more to please and occupy her, for he said that she might plant a maze at Versailles; that Mansart, the great architect, should design it according to her instructions, and that no one should interfere. That promise he did not quite manage to keep; there still exists a note to Mansart in the king's handwriting, which reads 'Let there be children everywhere', referring to the statues and fountains in Adelaide's maze.

77 & 78. Fountains in the maze and garden at Versailles

There were many treats enjoyed by them both; but to Adelaide, by far the greatest was to go hunting with the king in his open-carriage with its team of racing ponies, with children of her own age acting as postilions. The king did not ride to hounds after his operation; but he was an expert whip and drove at the gallop. Adelaide had complete trust in him and no fear. She loved the danger and, laughing, urged him on. To her he was the Sun King in very truth, the dispenser of gifts and kindness, the all-powerful and good magician who made a reality of fairyland. Her great gift to him was to love and support him, without asking for anything in return. She loved him too much to pester him with requests, and all through her short life did her best to make him cheerful. Shortly before she died, only sixteen years later, she overheard the king's daughters ridiculing her in whispers for bouncing around the king and talking baby-talk. 'I know as well as they do', she said to Mme de Saint-Simon, 'that I seem very silly and

79. *The wedding of the Duc de Bourgogne to Marie Adelaide of Savoy*

behave like an idiot; but he has to have a bustle about him, and that kind of thing distracts him.'

None of the mature women whom the king had loved had been so enthusiastic, so unselfish a partner in his private life and hobbies. Louise de La Vallière had deplored his desire for splendour. Glory to her was vanity, and the grandeur of Versailles a pointer to her sin and shame in being his mistress. Athénaïs, willing to share his glory and revelling in magnificence, thought only of personal advantage, encouraging his ideas for the wealth she hoped to extract from them. Françoise de Maintenon found Versailles pretty enough as a country house, but was shocked by the expense, and did not hesitate to tell him so. Only Adelaide saw in it a fairyland and in her old uncle the genius responsible for its creation. She became his ally, assistant and friend, using her charm to make the work run quickly and smoothly in the way that he liked. He increasingly thought her perfection, and Mme de Maintenon thought her not far short of that happy state. 'If any mischievous idea comes to her,' she said, 'I have only to say "that would be sinful", and she replies, "then I will not do it."'

Adelaide came into their lives at the very moment when they needed an outlet for parental love. The king, because of the terror he inspired in them, could find no object to cherish among his children and grandchildren. Mme de Maintenon's darling, the Duc du Maine, was twenty-six years old and no longer needed her, and they both sought in the little princess a child on whom to lavish the gentler, sweeter sides of their natures. This place in their hearts she filled to overflowing.

A year later, since there could be no doubt of Adelaide's fitness to be queen, they decided that she should be married, though for the time being in name only, to the Duc de Bourgogne on 7 December of the following year, 1697, soon after her twelfth birthday. The king looked forward with almost feverish excitement to the festivities, and let it be known that he hoped the Court would make glorious the great occasion by a display of rich and beautiful clothes. He himself, who, conscious of the nation's poverty, had for a long time past dressed very plainly, now ordered a number of the most costly and resplendent coats imaginable, and all sections of society, glad of the chance to be extravagant, vied with one another in magnificence and originality. The shops of Paris were soon emptied of rich silks, and gold and silver braid became virtually unprocurable. Everyone wanted new clothes; not only the nobility but quite unimportant townsfolk and lesser officials spent far more than they could afford and ran up huge debts. The king, who had given them the lead, soon repented of such wild extravagance. He could not understand, he said, how men could ruin themselves to supply their wives with finery—or indeed to obtain it for themselves. But it was too late, he had been taken at his word, and it was believed that privately he would not have wished it otherwise, for he took a great interest in fine stuffs and curious embroidery, and enjoyed praising the most beautiful and sumptuous of the costumes.

When the great day came, the wedding was celebrated with all due ceremony in the chapel at Versailles. Yet it was considered a dull day by the courtiers, for there had been another royal wedding in that year—the marriage of the Duc de Chartres to the king's daughter, Mlle de Blois, and the procession and details of this one were exactly similar. After the ceremony the king and his family dined in public, and on leaving the table he, with Monseigneur (the Grand Dauphin, father of the bridegroom) and all the ladies, went to see the bride undressed and put to bed. No man other than the king and his son were admitted to witness the *coucher*.

Shortly afterwards the bridegroom appeared and got into bed on the side opposite to the one where his bride was lying. Everyone then left the room, except Monseigneur who stayed, chatting with them pleasantly for about a quarter of an hour. He then told his son to rise, after first kissing his wife and bidding her goodnight. This last was an error of judgment. When the king heard of it he was much displeased, saying that he did not wish his grandson to kiss so much as the tip of

80. The Bassin d'Apollon, Versailles

his wife's little finger until the time came for them to live together.

There were two state balls to celebrate the occasion, a grand display of fireworks and a gala performance of an opera; but public rejoicings did not extend beyond Christmas, and no other balls were held that winter. There had been enough of extravagant spending.

One result of the royal marriage was the beginning of an attachment between the king and the fifteen-year-old Duc de Bourgogne, who had hitherto been too frightened to respond to any advances by his grandfather. He now began to show more confidence and the king, impressed by his goodwill and intelligence, took his training in statecraft into his own hands and began by appointing him to listen, as he had done, at meetings of the Council. In talking with him afterwards the king learned to respect his judgment, as the courtiers discovered when, against all custom, he was permitted to choose a man to be captain of his bodyguard. The king said, 'It is not right for me at my age to choose men who will serve me only a short time, but will be in your service for the rest of their lives.'

As he grew older, however, the king became increasingly exasperated by what even he considered to be the prince's altogether excessive and disruptive piety that tended to upset the life of the Court. He himself was strict in his observancies, never missing mass unless he was ill in bed, and rigorously keeping religious fasts to the extent of banning even fish on Good Friday; but the Duc de Bourgogne went much further. In 1701, when Adelaide recovered from an illness which he believed to have been a God-sent punishment for his own sins, he gave himself up to religious devotion, and drew away from the courtiers, refusing to take part in their pleasures unless some ceremony required his presence. He gave up dancing and playing cards in Lent; finally, he gave up gambling altogether, except for the lowest stakes. He was ashamed, he said, of the pleasure he felt in winning, and he ceased entirely to attend the ballet or the theatre, even when the king was present. He was, at that time, no ornament to the Court, and no pleasure to his merry young wife.

She provided the king's only solace in the disasters of the next decade; his delight in her constant companionship increased, for she studied his moods with never-failing tact. With her his youth returned, restored by her joyous enthusiasm when they hunted together behind his galloping ponies, sailed on the canal, or went walking to enjoy the flowers and fruit in the gardens of Versailles or Trianon. He rejoiced to find that she had intelligence and capabilities beyond all expectations; 'she is capable of difficult and important affairs,' he said, and he gave her the authority to appoint and control her own household, a responsibility bestowed on no other princess. He showered her with tokens of his love, and one favour which particularly moved her was an order to the master of his music to let his private orchestra play daily at the mass she attended, a delight for which she had never so much as hinted a desire. He came to lean on her for relief from the gloom of Mme de Maintenon and the austerity of the young Duc de Bourgogne, and he needed her more and more in the dreadful years ahead.

81. Louis XIV in his wheelchair en promenade

NAMUR PRIS PAR SA MAJESTÉ
LE DERNIER JUIN 1692

82. The siege of Namur, 1692

FAREWELL TO LOVE
AND GLORY

n 1700, there occurred the most important event in the reign of Louis XIV, precipitated by the long-awaited death of Charles II, the sickly King of Spain. Three weeks earlier, he had secretly made a will bequeathing the throne of Spain to one or other of the king's three grandsons, with an added clause to the effect that in case of a refusal the entire Spanish empire should be offered immediately to the Archduke Charles of Austria.

On 9 November, an officer arrived at Fontainebleau bearing news of King Charles's death and a copy of his will, which the king took and read with no change of expression and in perfect silence. He then spoke only to defer the day's shooting, announce a long period of Court mourning, and summon a meeting of his Council for three o'clock that same afternoon in Mme de Maintenon's room, for the purpose of deciding whether or not to accept the Spanish throne in the name of his grandson.

It was an agonizing decision, since acceptance would almost certainly provoke a European war, while a refusal would put Austria, France's most bitter enemy, on her northern and southern frontiers with only the unreliable Duchy of Savoy between them on the east. At the Council opinions were divided, and the king turned to Mme de Maintenon to ask what she advised. At first she hesitated because she dreaded a war; but seeing where her husband's wishes lay, she reluctantly opted for acceptance, although with the gravest misgivings. The result had never really been in doubt. Next day the king announced that he would accept, on behalf of his grandson the young Duc d'Anjou, the bequest of Spain and the undivided Spanish Empire.

The king was taking an appalling risk, but was not the risk worth taking? In past years French armies had everywhere been invincible, he had worthy marshals in Boufflers and Villars, and although his treasury had been seriously depleted by the Dutch wars and the fortunes spent in building sumptuous palaces and gardens, that could speedily be repaired, as Colbert had shown when, in so short a time, he had made France a rich and prosperous country. Moreover, God would inevitably be on his side in such a war, aimed at crushing the

Monr le Duc d'Anjou declaré par le Roy, et reconnu Roy d'Espagne à Versailles le 16. 9bre 1700

83. The Duc d'Anjou is recognized as the future King of Spain

heretical Dutch and English in order to leave Catholic France, with
Spain her satellite, absolute mistress of the Christian world. The path
of war led Louis XIV to seek glory unequalled since the time of the
Roman Emperors.

It was a disastrous resolve for France. The European nations,
although shocked and angered by Louis XIV's decision, did not
immediately resort to arms; but in 1701 the War of the Spanish
Succession broke out, which year after year brought crushing defeat
to the French armies. To Louis XIV and the French nation these
catastrophes appeared almost incredible; they could scarcely have
foreseen the effects of Marlborough's extraordinary genius, combined
with that of Prince Eugene, or have believed that the hitherto
invincible French armies would suffer defeats on the scale of
Blenheim, Ramillies, and Oudenarde. That these disasters would be
followed by the frost and famine that struck France in 1709, leaving
the country very near to bankruptcy and the people to starvation,
were events that could be attributed only to the wrath of God. That,
indeed, was the opinion of Mme de Maintenon. 'We must regard all
these happenings as the will of God,' she wrote to a friend. 'Our king
was too glorious; God humbles him so that he may be saved.' All her
misgivings regarding the succession had been realized; she was old, in
her seventies, and she daily had to bear the king's miseries and his
agonies of conscience, lest he be committing any mortal sin. She
longed to leave the Court, 'where only the old had good manners and
the young were perpetually drunk.' Her quiet rooms at Saint-Cyr
seemed like heaven to her; but she felt bound to the king by her
mission and could not leave him. It does not appear that she ever loved
him passionately, as in his selfish way he had always loved her; but
she gave him her complete devotion, although her chief concern was
always his salvation. She, to him, was a guide and confidante in whom

he reposed his trust, and though he used her unmercifully and disregarded her wishes whenever they went contrary to his own, he continued all his life to love and revere her. 'However much you may love me, my love for you will always be greater,' he had written to her from the army in 1691, and the few little scraps of notes preserved by the dames of Saint-Cyr tell of his deep affection.

None the less, he found her pessimism regarding the war hard to bear—she wrote to the same friend, in 1709, 'I think that we should bow to superior force and accept the chastisement of God (who is clearly not on our side). But it will not be my advice that settles the issue of peace and war.' Overwhelmed with work and worry, the king sought for any kind of amusement to lighten his leisure hours and he was finding his wife's pious prudery something of a trial. Thus while he supported before the Court her tremendous dignity, he could not help enjoying the naughty tricks which the young Duchesse de Bourgogne played on her, to put her out of countenance.

Louvois, the minister for war, had died in 1691; and for the past eighteen years Louis XIV had himself filled that office. He was no mere figurehead, but read and signed all orders to his armies. No move might be made without his prior consent, and his generals complained that while couriers were galloping to and from Versailles, seeking his permission, opportunities were lost. In the terrible years of defeat, he devoted himself every day, and well into the night, to the task of supervising his commanders. His leisure hours were much reduced, and he felt the strain and increasing exhaustion. He gave himself up to saving France, and his subjects, it was his conviction, were in bounden duty to sacrifice everything so that he might enjoy his rare times of relaxation, and be pleased to accompany and divert him, if so required, whether or not they were in the mood. To obstruct him at such times was, in his eyes, outrageous ingratitude.

This was the cause of his outburst of rage, in public, against his pet the little Duchesse de Bourgogne, in the summer of 1708. He had planned to take her to Marly, because he delighted in her company. But she was pregnant, and the doctors said unfit to travel, which enraged him, for he had been used to his mistresses accompanying him even when they were ill or just risen from childbed, always caparisoned in stiff Court dress and proclaiming themselves perfectly well. He angrily agreed to deferring the excursion for a few days, but insisted that well or ill, the princess should accompany him on the following Wednesday. This she did, but after two days at Marly she had a miscarriage. The king was given the news in the garden and turned to tell the courtiers the bare facts. There were murmurs of compassion, and of distress, since she had miscarried several times

84. Details from a contemporary engraving showing the effects of the winter of 1709

before and might have no more children. At this the king completely lost his temper. 'Why should I care?' he loudly exclaimed. 'She has a son already, has she not? And is not the Duc de Berry [her husband's brother] of an age to marry and have children? Thank God this has happened! At last I can come and go as I please and not be thwarted by the doctors.' His hearers were horrified to hear him. Saint-Simon says that there was a silence in which one might have heard an ant walking. Stupefaction reigned, and his atrocious words had repercussions far beyond the Court at Marly.

The courtiers were dismayed, not only by the king's inhumanity, but because they truly believed that Adelaide was his only remaining distraction, and the thought of her falling out of favour filled them with alarm.

So indeed did his outburst, for it was his fixed policy never to show his feelings, but in joy or grief to maintain the same unshakeable calm. Foscarini, the Venetian ambassador, had written to the Doge some years back of this admirable quality, adding that it remained to be seen whether Louis XIV would be able to 'maintain his pose of noble indifference' if fortune turned against him to the extent of destroying not only his happiness but also his glory. That, indeed, was to be the king's fate, for public disasters were succeeded by private griefs; yet his outburst over Adelaide proved to be an isolated incident. He remained apparently unmoved throughout all his subsequent sorrows, and his courage did not fail. He was a man of steel, except in his almost abject fear of mortal sin.

That side of his character he showed only to his wife, and to his aged confessor Père de La Chaise, whom none the less he treated with total lack of consideration. That good old man was more than eighty years old, gentle, decrepit, altogether broken down; he constantly begged for retirement, but the king who found him a comfort would not hear of that, sending a carriage to fetch him at any hour of the day or night if he felt the urgent need for confession and absolution. After the old man's death, in 1709, the king's praise of him was above all for his kindness. 'He was so kind,' he said smiling, 'that I used sometimes to scold him for it; but his reply was always the same, "It is not I who am kind, but you who are so cruel."' Saint-Simon relates that the listening courtiers were shocked and lowered their eyes.

He was living under a fearful strain. The war dragged on, and the disastrous frosts and famine of 1709 brought his kingdom to the very edge of bankruptcy and starvation, but that year, in fact, represented the lowest point in the fortunes of suffering France, and thereafter the tide began to turn. In the early days of 1712, the Maréchal de Villars won a great victory at Denain that averted total collapse; for had he

85. The Grand Dauphin and his family

been defeated, there were no more troops to prevent the invasion of France and the taking of Paris.

Before the battle, the king wrote to Villars, 'Should your army be defeated, what ought I to do? Retire to Blois as many people advise? But my army can surely not be so crushed as to make them incapable of standing firm on the Somme. If there should be a disaster, write to me; I will then collect all the men I can find in Paris, and go to Peronne or Saint-Quentin to die beside you, or save our country.'

Villars won the battle, and a few weeks later a conference was held at Utrecht, followed by the signing of peace in 1713. France was able to recover from the calamities of the war and famine, but not to regain the dominance of Europe. The Sun King's military glory was a thing of the past.

On him, fate had other blows still to inflict, as death struck down one member of the royal family after another. In 1711, his son, Monseigneur, le Grand Dauphin, died suddenly. Then, in the following year, death struck again, this time to destroy virtually his whole family.

143

On 18 January 1712, the king, still in mourning for his son, removed his Court to Marly. Adelaide, now by inheritance Dauphine of France, was suffering from a bad bout of toothache and went to bed as soon as they arrived; but she got up in the evening to preside over the salon. Next day she was better and on 1 February was able to return to Versailles with the king and Mme de Maintenon, who were not much disturbed because she was newly pregnant, a state that frequently caused her gums to be inflamed and her temperature to rise. At noon on that day she ate a large dinner, with a rich cake she had cooked herself, and washed it down with a glass of mulled wine to prevent indigestion. That night she went to bed with a raging fever and a violent pain in her face which opium did nothing to relieve. In the following days and nights the fever and the pain persisted and she grew ever weaker. It was then that the new Dauphin, her husband, who had been with her all the time, was persuaded to go to his room for fear of contagion, and Mme de Maintenon took his place, leaving her only when the king came.

The doctors treated her according to the fashion of the times, with copious bleedings and powerful emetics which destroyed her remaining strength. She died a week later, on the evening of 11 February, in Mme de Maintenon's loving arms.

The king and his old wife drove straight to Marly to be alone in their grief, both of them weeping so bitterly that they could not summon up the strength even to visit the Dauphin. The king, indeed, was stricken down with misery, the only piercing sorrow that ever entered his life. To the King of Spain he wrote, 'I have lost a daughter in the Dauphine, and although you know how dearly I have always loved her, you cannot imagine my misery at her loss . . . There will never come a moment when I do not miss her.'

Saint-Simon, living at the Court, says, 'With her death all joy vanished, all pleasures, entertainments and diversions were overcast and darkness covered the face of the Court. She had been its life and light . . . , and if, after her death, the court continued to subsist, it merely lingered on . . . No princess was ever so sincerely mourned, none more worth regretting. Indeed mourning for her has never ceased, a secret, involuntary sadness has remained, a terrible emptiness that never can be filled.'

But there was more to come. The Dauphin, heartbroken, and sickening with the same illness that had attacked his wife, joined the king at Marly three days later. He looked so ill and so alarmingly pale that the doctors took his pulse, but found no cause for alarm. On the following day, however, a rash appeared and he was clearly very ill. Having no strength left, and no will to live, he died on the morning of 18 February, just a week after his wife's death.

Strange to say, he was fulfilling his own prophecy. Two years earlier, a fortune-teller from Turin had predicted that the Dauphine would die before her twenty-seventh birthday, and she had asked the prince, in jest, whom he would take for his second wife, when she had left him a widower. 'If that should ever happen,' he replied, 'I should never marry again. In a week's time I should follow you to the grave.'

His death, though not the king's greatest grief, was probably a greater shock. He had become personally attached to him, but the loss of their Dauphin was a blow to the whole nation. Never had an heir to the throne of France shown more promise or aroused higher hopes than this serious, godly, intelligent young prince, whom the king himself was training for the succession. Nor had there been any doubt in the minds of most Frenchmen that his charming, kindly young wife would make a worthy queen. Mme de Maintenon wrote, 'The king is overwhelmed with grief, and the whole of France is stunned.'

The deaths, having been so tragic and so sudden, inevitably aroused rumours of poisoning, and stories were told of a beautiful snuffbox, given to the Dauphine on the day of her return to Versailles, which had subsequently mysteriously vanished and was nowhere to be found. The rumours intensified after the Dauphin's death, but when three weeks later their children, Louis XIV's great-grandsons, the five-year-old Duc de Bretagne and his two-year-old brother, the Duc d'Anjou, both fell desperately ill with high fever accompanied by a rash, little doubt remained that the cause of their parents' deaths had been measles, of which there had been an outbreak in Paris. Other members of the royal family had also caught the illness; Monsieur le Duc, for example, had been seriously indisposed at Marly, and the Dauphin and Dauphine had both visited him.

When the little Duc de Bretagne's temperature rose to an alarming degree the doctors seized on him to bleed, purge, and administer emetics; but despite—or because of—their ministrations he died. Madame did not believe in doctors and was of the second opinion. 'They opened a vein', she wrote, 'and in consequence of this operation the poor child died.' The younger prince, a frail and sickly infant, was snatched away by his governess and locked up in her bedroom. She kept him warm, and firmly refused to hand him over to the doctors who wished to bleed him also. Thanks to her care and against all expectation he recovered to become Louis XV on his great-grandfather's death.

The king was indeed crushed by the continued blows of an inexorable fate; but somehow he contrived to fulfil his public duties apparently unmoved. He read and wrote dispatches, presided over his Council, gave audiences, held receptions. Saint-Simon, himself broken-hearted, joined him as he walked in the gardens, 'but the wretchedness of seeing him look almost as usual drove me quickly away. At that time, as never before,' Saint-Simon added, 'he deserved the title of Louis the Great.'

In private he wept again and again; but found in Mme de Maintenon a rock of loving support. In the past she had cared only for his salvation, and had been lavish with criticism and reproaches. Now she showed her deep affection for him, caring for his health as a good wife should, and doing her best to console him. On 27 March she wrote, 'the king does all he can to support his strength, but again and again his grief returns, and sharing it as I do, my own misery is increased. Yet his health does not fail, and he neglects none of his duties.'

Those who saw her with the king could not forbear to admire her. Even Madame, her most vicious detractor, was moved to write, 'Although the old baggage is our worst enemy, I wish her a long life for the king's sake, since everything would be ten times worse were she to die now. He so adores her that without her he would not long survive, and I therefore hope that she will live a long time yet.'

In those sad days Versailles was a place of mourning. The king, who disliked long faces, did his best to be cheerful but was unsuccessful. He

87. Louis XIV
giving audience to his subjects

88. The Chapel, Versailles

invited guests to Marly, played billiards, attended concerts and even plays; he also became more tolerant, allowing the courtiers to smoke, a habit of which he disapproved. But he remembered that he had forbidden the little Dauphine to smoke, although it was said to relieve her toothache, and at the thought of her he was often overcome. Mme de Maintenon was apt to change the subject when the names of the Dauphin and Dauphine were mentioned; but the king was always complaining that there were no longer any young people at his Court. In 1712, there was no great work in progress at Versailles to occupy his creative energies; but he still enjoyed working with his gardeners, and one recently finished and magnificent edifice, the splendid chapel designed by Mansart, filled him with pride.

When the château was being rebuilt and enlarged, there had been no plans made for a chapel. One of the rooms leading from the state apartments had been arranged as a temporary measure for the celebration of mass and other church services. It was only when the new century drew near that Louis XIV awakened to the thought that God had not been given his rightful place in the building of the seat of government. The year 1699 was not a good time to embark on costly building, for the wars had emptied the treasury of France, and the people suffered under crippling taxation. None the less the king, eager to please God, truly religious, but also delighted with the opportunity

147

to indulge his passion for architectural planning, had proceeded without delay to gather together the materials for a magnificent structure which was not finished until 1709.

One might imagine that Mme de Maintenon, in her zealous piety, would have urged the king on to such a holy endeavour. But it was not so. At that time, and throughout the first disastrous decade of the century, her mind was full of the sufferings and poverty of the French people under crippling taxation. Mlle d'Aumale, her secretary, writes that 'she did everything in her power to oppose the building of the magnificent chapel which the king was building at Versailles because the people's poverty was very great at that time; moreover, she did not believe that Versailles would for much longer be the king's residence. But he was absolutely determined and her protests were unavailing.'

It was Jean Hardouin Mansart, appointed on 8 January 1699 to be superintendent of works and buildings, who incited the king to embark on the long and hugely costly enterprise. Saint-Simon, who despised and disliked him, says that, eaten up by ambition and the love of money, and knowing the king's passionate delight in building, he so tempted him with alluringly beautiful projects, that the money was instantly forthcoming.

Mansart did not live to see the work finished, or to hear the chorus of praise that greeted his achievement, for he died very suddenly in 1708, leaving the chapel to be completed by his brother-in-law, Robert de Cotte.

On 23 April 1710 the king entered the choir to hear the singing of a motet and judge the acoustics. He pronounced himself to be perfectly satisfied and, on 8 June of that same year, Cardinal de Noailles, the Archbishop of Paris, consecrated the building, and the king prayed there for the first time. After his dinner, he returned to hear vespers.

Unlike Mme de Maintenon, he was not unduly perturbed by the huge expense at a time when France was poverty-stricken and many of his subjects starving. He was filled with joy at the beauty of the gold and white church, which, at that time (two years before death had mown down the majority of his descendants) he intended to be the

89. A violinist in the king's ensemble

Mᵗ le Colonel et officiers de la Ville
Tambours de la
grande Ecurie
les haut bois de la grande Ecurie 27 mᵉʳˢ les huissiers Audianciers du Chastelet Mᵉˢ les Greffiers du Chastelet.
mᵉ les Capitaines des trois cents Archers ou Garde de la Ville

mᵉ les Commissaires huissiers de l'hotel de Ville.
le Roy D'Armes Mᵉˢ les Magistrats Conseillers Procureur du Roy et Commissaires
du Chastelet

Les Trompettes de
la grande Ecurie du Roy.
Mᵉˢ les Septheraults d'Armes publiant la Paix. messieurs les magistrats de l'hotel de Ville.

90. *The procession preceding the signing of the Treaty of Utrecht*

temple of Saint-Louis, the shrine of a Bourbon dynasty. Despite his sorrow, he took comfort as his own death approached from having offered to God, in the face of every conceivable obstruction, this glorious token of his faith.

When, in 1713, the Treaty of Utrecht was signed, it brought peace to France on far more advantageous terms than could ever have been expected. Although the captured Dutch fortresses were returned to Holland and the Spanish Empire was dismembered, Louis XIV's grandson remained on the Spanish throne, which had been the king's prime object for going to war. As the months passed, his spirits rose and he began once more to enjoy life. The Dauphine's death had caused him piercing grief, but it was not in his nature to harbour melancholy. He was seventy-five years old in 1713, but still in excellent health; he continued to enjoy an afternoon's hunting or shooting, on foot or in his pony-carriage, and on one occasion succeeded in bringing down thirty-two pheasants with thirty-four shots. In the evenings, in Mme de Maintenon's room, his four-and-twenty violins played the music he loved, and sometimes there was community-singing, with the king joining in the choruses of his favourite drinking-songs. Best of all, to him, was the opera, a diversion of which Mme de Maintenon strongly disapproved. 'It is his only genuine pleasure,' she wrote, 'but one hears nothing there except what is totally opposed to the teaching of the Gospels . . . It is true that he does not mind the immorality; he cares only for the beauty of the music and its harmonies.'

149

One other source of real pleasure the king possessed was the quiet bliss of domestic happiness with Mme de Maintenon, to whom he had been married for nearly thirty years. She made him happy and he loved her more as she grew older. She noticed the change in him and remarked on it in several of her letters. 'He seems to me to be happier than I have ever known him.' It was not so with her, however. In 1713 she was seventy-eight years old, and miserable at becoming hard of hearing. 'I can hardly see now,' she wrote to a crony in Spain, 'and am even more deaf. What I say is barely intelligible because I mumble now that my teeth are gone.' This piteous portrait may have been true but Mme de Maintenon's mind was not failing, she merely wished people to believe that she needed to retire from public life.

Thus she never ceased complaining. In another letter, this time from Marly: 'If I stay here much longer,' she says, 'I shall be crippled for life. None of the windows or doors will stay shut, and the wind reminds me of the hurricanes in America.' She had a shelter specially constructed (' *ma niche* ') to put around her chair—high screens lined with crimson damask, to protect her from the fresh air which she dreaded but which the king thought invigorating. There is no doubt that he did not put himself out for her comfort; but in their last years together he showed her more tenderness and relied on her more than ever for spiritual guidance and practical advice. She never failed him, and she made him happy; but she did not love him, for this extraordinary woman, although she could give her heart to small children, appears to have been incapable of loving any adult. After the king's death, she confided to Mlle de Glapion, 'When everyone thought me the luckiest woman on earth, the very opposite was true.' But though she never ceased to ask for pity from her friends, when the king came to her she was full of good cheer, intent only on his amusement.

For the next two years Louis XIV remained in good health and enjoyed an active life; hunting three days a week; reviewing the household troops, a ceremony he vastly enjoyed; working with ministers; giving audience to ambassadors and marshals of France; receiving the artists and learned men who gathered at his Court; spending his evenings chatting and listening to the orchestra in Mme de Maintenon's room.

The first signs of illness appeared on 10 August, in the summer of 1715, when he was seventy-seven years old. On the previous day he

91. A concert in the fifth chamber, Versailles

92. Louis XIV with his heirs and the Duchesse de Ventadour

had returned exhausted from hunting and people had remarked on his looking gravely ill. On the 11th, he seemed much as usual, held Council in the morning and later walked to the Trianon gardens which he so much loved. He never went out again.

On the 14th he went to hear mass in the new chapel, for the last time. He still continued to preside over the meetings of the Council and to eat his supper in public. On Tuesday, the 19th, he had agonizing pain in his left leg, and it became apparent that gangrene had set in. He was sleeping very badly; but he held a Council of State, received foreign ambassadors at dinner, and went immediately afterwards to Mme de Maintenon's room to work with the Chancellor and, in the evening, to hear a concert.

No remedies were applied until too late, for Fagon his old doctor refused to admit that the illness was serious, and Mme de Maintenon took the same line. The king himself remained unconvinced; but because of his friendship for Fagon and his faith in Mme de Maintenon he took no action. He had had an iron constitution; but his strength had been sapped by the persistent purging, bleeding, and sweating (against the gout) inflicted upon him by the doctors in accordance with the pernicious practice of that time.

Sunday, 25 August, was the feast of Saint-Louis, and the night before had been very bad. No secret was now made of grave danger to his life; but the king would allow no change in the usual arrangements for that day. The drums and fifes stationed beneath his windows struck up a tune when he awoke, and his twenty-four violins and oboes played in the ante-room while he was at dinner. That was the last time that he dined in public, saying to those who tried to dissuade him, 'I have lived among the people of my Court, and I wish to die among them. They have followed me during the entire course of my life; it is only right that they should see the end.'

By that time liquids were all that he could swallow, and when the doctors came to examine his legs they found black marks and were thrown into confusion. They had been giving him milk to drink, and quinine in water. Now both were cancelled; but no one knew what to do next. Finally they admitted that he had only a little time left in which to prepare for death.

Mme de Maintenon, the Duc du Maine and the Chancellor then came to him and he signed a codicil to his will, giving his bastards, the Duc du Maine and the Comte de Toulouse, greater power in the next reign. This codicil was later abolished by the Parlement, and Saint-Simon, who hated and suspected Mme de Maintenon, thought it 'a wicked advantage taken of the king in his extremity because she and her darling M. du Maine believed that not enough had been done for them in his will . . . It shows', he said, 'the lengths to which unbridled ambition will lead people.'

After the deed was done, Mme de Maintenon sent for the ladies and

93. Cheating at cards

the music; but their chatter so tired the king that he fell asleep. When he awoke, his mind was in such confusion, and his pulse so weak, that they took fright and called the doctors, who decided that the time had come to appeal for the last rites.

There was a delay of a quarter of an hour while his confessor was summoned, and Cardinal de Rohan went to the chapel for the Host. Mme de Maintenon made use of the time to ensure that the king should omit nothing in his confession. According to Mlle d'Aumale, 'she reminded him of several incidents which she had herself witnessed, in order that he should not forget to ask God's forgiveness for them all . . . The king', she added, 'was grateful to Mme de Maintenon and thanked her.'

The next days and nights were very painful. The gangrene spread up his leg and above his knee, and the pain was intolerable. He was so weak that he could not lift his head to drink. None the less, he used the time to bid farewell to his family and his courtiers, as well as to the little Dauphin, who was brought by Mme de Ventadour to his bedside, a repetition of the scene when Louis XIV, at the age of four, presented himself for the last time to be embraced by his dying father.

There was one more thing to be done, before the king could rest in peace, and that was the destruction of his private papers. It was then that he and Mme de Maintenon together burned all but a few of their letters. Mlle d'Aumale records that amongst the papers they came on copies of the guest-lists for Marly, which made the king smile and say, 'We can burn all this, it is only rubbish.' They also found one of his rosaries, which he gave her, saying very gently, 'I will give you this, not as a relic, but just as a souvenir.'

'He said goodbye to me three times,' wrote Mme de Maintenon on a sheet of paper enclosed with her will. 'The first time, he assured me that his only regret was in leaving me; but, he said sighing, "we shall soon meet again." I entreated him to think only of God. The second time, he asked my forgiveness for not having made me happy; but said that he had indeed always loved and esteemed me. Then, feeling that he was near weeping, he asked me to see that we were not overheard, and added, "But no one could be surprised at my being moved by love for you." On the third occasion, he said, "What will become of you? You have nothing." I again exhorted him to think only of God; then, reflecting that I did not know how the princes would treat me, I begged him to recommend me to the Duc d'Orléans.' This the king did, and, in the event, she was treated with great generosity, with her future, at Saint-Cyr, where she longed to retire, guaranteed for the rest of her life.

On the following day he was in less pain and appeared a little to

revive. To Père Tellier his confessor, who asked if his sufferings were very great, he replied, 'Well! no, and that is what disturbs me. I could wish to suffer more for the expiation of my sins.' In the evening, however, there was a relapse, and no hope remained.

Mme de Maintenon left the king's room with her black hood drawn over her face and, led by the Maréchal de Villeroy, went past the doors of her apartment, which she did not enter, and down the grand staircase. At the foot, she drew back her veil—'dry-eyed', says Saint-Simon—embraced Villeroy, saying 'Adieu, Monsieur le Maréchal,' and stepping into the king's coach, which she always used, drove away to Saint-Cyr.

But Saint-Simon is not to be trusted when dealing with those whom he hated as he hated Mme de Maintenon. He may well have been unjust to her, since it is reported that before leaving she insisted on her confessor seeing the king, who had lost consciousness, in order to be sure that she could do no more for him, and that the priest had returned saying, 'You may leave him now; he has no further want of you.' She was eighty years old, and under an enormous strain; Mlle d'Aumale may have been nearer the truth in saying, 'She left Versailles before the king's death, fearing lest, in his last moments, she might give way to tears.'

Soon after her departure, however, the king recovered consciousness and asked for her. She returned to him in a hurry; but when he again relapsed into a coma she drove quickly back to Saint-Cyr, and was there when he died. Saint-Simon gleefully wrote, 'No more need to fear the old witch, her wicked wand is broken and she is back where she began—no more than the old widow Scarron.'

That, too, is grossly unfair. Mme de Maintenon had been a rock of support to the king in his last years (he called her 'Your Solidity'), and had given him what all his life he had yearned for, the pleasure and warmth of family affection. Mme de Sévigné, who had been her friend in earlier days, describes her as being 'the soul of honesty'. She was frigid, according to Fénelon, and incapable of married love; but she did sincerely believe that God had made it her first duty to steer the king away from mortal sin. She had succeeded, but it had been no easy task.

The greatest joy in her life was her school at Saint-Cyr, and it was there that she died peacefully, in comfortable retirement, on 15 April 1719. If she truly believed that by forgetting the world she would herself be forgotten, a visit that she received in 1717 must have shaken her considerably. On 11 June of that year, Peter the Great, Tsar of all the Russias, announced his intention of calling on her. Mme de Maintenon immediately retired to bed, fearing the fatigue of

155

ceremonial and Court attire. After he had gone, she wrote to her cousin Mme de Caylus describing what happened.

'The Tsar arrived at seven o'clock. He asked me through the interpreter if I were ill. I said that I was. He then asked the nature of my illness. "Extreme old age," I replied, "and bodily weakness." He found no answer to that, and his interpreter appeared not to hear me very well. It was a very short visit. He is still somewhere in the building, but I am not sure where. I forgot to say that he had the curtains of my bed drawn back in order to have a good look at me. Let us hope that his curiosity was satisfied. Goodnight dear cousin, I am just about to drink my milk.'

Early in 1719, aware that her strength had begun to fail, she burned her few remaining letters from the king, and turned her attention to the making of her will. She died quietly, at peace with herself and with God, on the evening of 15 April.

'She told me many times,' said Mlle d'Aumale, her secretary, 'that she longed for death, and could not believe that after all the Grace He had shown her, God would wish to condemn her. I sometimes said that I feared the wrath of God and to be in Hell. "Good Heavens! How can you imagine such a thing?" she exclaimed. "An idea like that never enters my head . . . I have done my best, and I feel that is all God requires of us. No! I find it impossible to believe that he will damn me."'

Louis XIV, on his deathbed, had not been so certain of God's tolerance. In those terrible last days, when he lay dying in agony, he confessed to having spent millions on the building and decoration of his palaces while his people starved, and to causing the deaths of thousands of his subjects in unnecessary wars, for his glory's sake. Yet there was another side to his nature. He took no pleasure in inflicting pain for its own sake; he was not revengeful, and he was often kind, a word he used frequently in his memoirs. Saint-Simon, who knew and disliked him, said, 'He was born good and just. God endowed him with the makings of a good, even perhaps of a great king. All the wickedness in him came from without.'

Voltaire, who was twenty-one years old when Louis XIV died, and belonged to a later generation, said of him, 'They will not speak of him without respect, nor will his name ever fail to bring to mind the thought of an unforgettable age.'

St Denis en France

Mont-Martre

Le Clerge de S.t Denis

Carosse de Madame
la Regente

Officiers de la Maison
du Roy

Carosse de Madame la Douairiere

Les Gentils homme de la maison
du Roy

Pages de la grande et
petit Ecurie du Roy

Carosse de Mons.r le Regent
Duc d'Orleans

Carosse du Roy

Les Escuyer
du Roy

Corps du Roy

Gardes du Corps
du Roy

Ausmoniers du Roy avec
les Herauts d'Armes aux 4.
coings du Corps

Chez J. Chiquet a Paris   *Les Cents Suisses*

95. *The funeral procession of Louis XIV*

INDEX

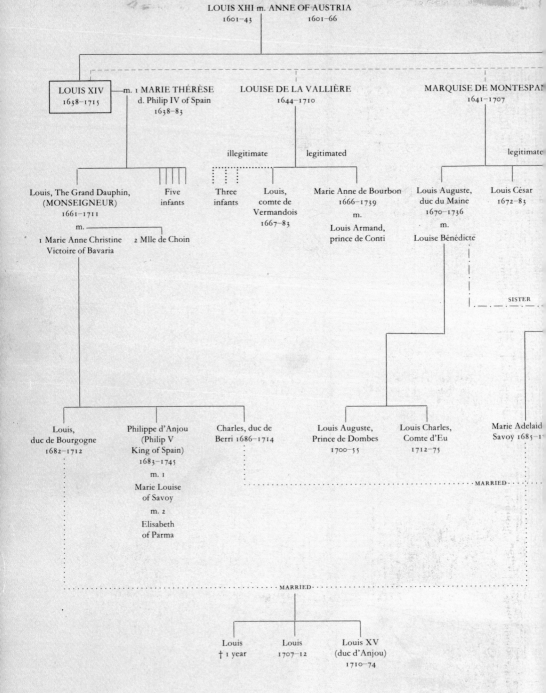

LOUIS XIII m. ANNE OF AUSTRIA
1601–43   1601–66

LOUIS XIV — m. 1 MARIE THÉRÈSE   LOUISE DE LA VALLIÈRE   MARQUISE DE MONTESPAN
1638–1715   d. Philip IV of Spain   1644–1710   1641–1707
                    1638–83

                                        illegitimate   legitimated   legitimate

Louis, The Grand Dauphin,   Five   Three   Louis,   Marie Anne de Bourbon   Louis Auguste,   Louis César
(MONSEIGNEUR)   infants   infants   comte de   1666–1739   duc du Maine   1672–83
1661–1711   Vermandois   m.   1670–1736
                                                              1667–83   Louis Armand,   m.
m. ——————————————   prince de Conti   Louise Bénédicte
1 Marie Anne Christine   2 Mlle de Choin
Victoire of Bavaria

                                                                                                                            SISTER

Louis,   Philippe d'Anjou   Charles, duc de   Louis Auguste,   Louis Charles,   Marie Adelaide
duc de Bourgogne   (Philip V   Berri 1686–1714   Prince de Dombes   Comte d'Eu   Savoy 1685–1
1682–1712   King of Spain)   1700–55   1712–75
                    1683–1745
                    m. 1
                    Marie Louise
                    of Savoy
                    m. 2
                    Elisabeth   MARRIED
                    of Parma

                                        MARRIED

                    Louis   Louis   Louis XV
                    † 1 year   1707–12   (duc d'Anjou)
                                                  1710–74

Design for a table to be made at the Gobelins